GW01179592

THE EVOLUTION OF ORTEGA Y GASSET AS LITERARY CRITIC

Demetrios Basdekis

State University of New York
College at Oneonta

UNIVERSITY
PRESS OF
AMERICA

LANHAM • NEW YORK • LONDON

Copyright © 1986 by

University Press of America,® Inc.

4720 Boston Way
Lanham, MD 20706

3 Henrietta Street
London WC2E 8LU England

All rights reserved

Printed in the United States of America

Library of Congress Cataloging in Publication Data

Basdekis, Demetrios, 1930-
  The evolution of Ortega y Gasset as literary critic.

  Bibliography: p.
  1. Ortega y Gasset, José, 1883-1955—Knowledge—
literature.   I. Title.
PQ6627.R8Z6   1986   809   86-22396
ISBN 0-8191-5667-1 (alk. paper)
ISBN 0-8191-5668-X (pbk. : alk. paper)

All University Press of America books are produced on acid-free
paper which exceeds the minimum standards set by the National
Historical Publications and Records Commission.

ACKNOWLEDGMENTS

This will acknowledge my debt to the late Paul Collins, as well as to Professor Anthony Roda, both of Oneonta, philosophers in the Socratic tradition, for the time given to the informal discussion of problems relating to the preparation of this study, as well as for their generosity in allowing me access to their private libraries.

Special thanks are also due Ciriaco Morón Arroyo, Hinchliff Professor of Hispanic Studies at Cornell University, without whose guidance, advice, and generosity this study would have been impossible.

Last but not least, my sincere gratitude to Susan Lapine for the meticulous care and hard work put into the preparation of this manuscript.

For
Georgia, Theodoros, Athanasios

TABLE OF CONTENTS

CHAPTER I

THE SOCIO-HUMAN PHASE

In his comprehensive study of José Ortega y Gasset (1883-1955), the eminent humanist Ciriaco Morón Arroyo identifies four distinct stages in the evolution of Ortega as writer and thinker, pinpointing as crucial turning points in the latter's development as philosopher the years 1907, 1914, 1920, and 1927.[1]

This present essay on Ortega as literary critic is an attempt to clarify his practical criticism against the philosophical and methodological backgrounds which characterize these stages of development and their primary sources of inspiration as identified by Morón Arroyo, with the slight modification that I shall treat stages two and three of Ortega's philosophical development - the phenomenological and the biological, respectively - as a single critical perspective.

Even some years prior to Ortega's well-known Marburg or Neo-Kantian period (1907-11) - the period which prefaces his definitive immersion into the phenomenologies of Husserl and Scheler (1913)[2] - Ortega had demonstrated, through his youthful writings on esthetics, as well as through his practical criticism, that his approach to literature was originally guided by an ideal norm that demanded "human art," an apparently far cry from the conviction which subsequently culminated in the pronouncements in 1924 that genuine art is intrinsically inhuman, that in order to qualify as art it must be dehumanized.

There is, then, adequate evidence that "human art," together with its moral and social implications, was a significant factor in Ortega's criticism some years before the norm became more obvious under the tutelage of the Marburg masters Herman Cohen and Paul Natorp, when the moral ideal in art became more rigid, and more closely allied to the Kantian ethical ideal of morality as obligation.

It is not unreasonable to suspect that the presence of the social and moral norms in the articles published by Ortega between 1902 and 1906 was first inspired by the work of the French esthetician Jean Marie Guyau, whose widely-read L'Art au point de vue sociologique (1890) saw at least four editions in Paris alone just a few years following its publication. As early as 1899, Azorín, whose work Ortega certainly knew at the turn of the century, had published, as part of a longer treatise on criticism, the article "Sociological Criticism,"[3] which is a precis of the popular work of Guyau, while by 1902, a Spanish edition of Guyau was already circulating in Madrid.[4]

In any case, in this context, it is interesting to note that while Ortega mentions Guyau only once in his complete works, and this not until 1924, he reveals a close prior knowledge of the sociological esthetics of the thinker whom he refers to as "the genial Frenchman Guyau."[5] And while Ortega concludes that Guyau's death prevented him from developing his unusual insights adequately, he stresses the point that the idea of art from a sociological point of view was a seminal one, latent with future potential, notwithstanding the fact that Ortega then proceeds to invert Guyau's social perspective for a purpose which clearly contradicts the idealism of the French thinker, for the purpose of demonstrating that art is fundamentally asocial. As I hope to demonstrate, Ortega had also radically inverted, between 1913 and 1924, his own early thinking with respect to the social and moral values of art, with respect to "human art."

Yet whether or not Ortega's single discussion of Guyau is as indicative of his youthful debt to the French philosopher as I think it is, the fact of the matter is that the esthetic pronouncements of the early Ortega do indeed parallel Guyau's socio-moralistic dogma on the ideal function of literature, especially as this appears in his most widely-disseminated book: Guyau's central premise is that art should nurture the moral awareness necessary for the human community to thrive in collective harmony. His favorite targets are Verlaine, Baudelaire, and the symbolists in general, for these culprits are unbalanced decadents whose pessimism and glorification of base instincts represent a serious threat to the health of the community. It is therefore understandable, according to Guyau, that being as they are amoral, the art of these social decadents is characterized by their maniacal devotion to form. There is constant reference in Guyau to the "reign of brutality" which typifies the literature of his contemporaries, including the literature of base instincts represented by the work of Zola, where trivialism is often confused with realism.

A similar view of literature, both implicit and explicit, can be detected in the earliest of Ortega's articles, particularly in the articles on his contemporaries, the talented Spanish modernists, many of whom owed a substantial debt to French literature.

Before marching off to Marburg in November of 1906, beginning in 1902, at the age of nineteen, Ortega published in Madrid journals seven articles which center on either specific literary figures or on general literary topics.[6] The most salient common denominator of all these early efforts is their distinct ethico-social thrust, their rather frenetic appeal for a literature which would help civilize a rather decadent Spanish community. Thus, for example, the very first of these articles,

2

"Personal Criticism," decidedly abrasive, replete with half-developed, fragmentary ideas, concludes that personal criticism is desirable because the amorphous masses - a theme destined to return time and again - need moral direction by strong leaders who know how to assert themselves with respect to right and wrong.

It is in the most significant of these early articles, "Maxims" (1906), a lengthy review in which Ortega censures a group of Spanish modernist poets for their excessive dedication to sonorous estheticism, that Ortega sounds most like the moralist Guyau: after stating that the way he sees things is diametrically opposed to the way the new poets see things, he excoriates them for their decadence, their narcissism, their exclusive dedication to the word itself, and their ivory tower preciosity achieved at the expense of human and national concern. The essay in question amounts to a call for engaged, or "human" literature as opposed to mannerism.7

Among the articles under discussion, the one dealing with one of the <u>Sonatas</u> of the most brilliant prose formalist of his generation, Ramón del Valle Inclán, is eloquent testimony of a young Ortega at his analytic best. Published in 1904, this article acknowledges the fact that Valle Inclán is a peerless master of exquisite Castilian. It stresses the artist's uniqueness, as well as his unquestionable role as an innovator of language, and focuses on the mechanics of the use of such language as the key to Valle Inclán's superb style. Yet notwithstanding the superlatives bestowed on a rather decadent Spaniard - rare praise, it should be stressed -, Ortega concludes that the absence of the transcendental dimension in Valle Inclán is the one deficiency which prevents him from being a truly great artist, and ends his essay with a plea to this great modernist that he opt for things more "decidedly human" than exquisite princesses, and that he abandon his mania for boasting as well. Once again, although this early effort does indeed foreshadow the more typical critical Ortega of the future, the one who would approach art from a strictly formal perspective, the socio-human criterion is still paramount.

Two more pieces from this same year (1904) of Ortega's pre-Marburg period are of additional interest with respect to the early extra-literary focus of his criticism. The first of these, "The Poet of Mystery," which I shall discuss at greater length in a separate chapter on poetry and theater, is a disquisition into the work of the Belgian symbolist Maurice Maeterlinck, while the second, "An Exuberant Countenance," is an enthusiastic reaction to a book by the French writer Ana de Noailles.

Ana de Noailles is generously extolled for what amounts to a virtuous optimism; a positive, joyful fascination in the presence of all things in life. It is no great surprise, Ortega interjects at one point in his article, that women in France are beginning to surpass men as writers, since the latters' spirit has been corroded by a decadence which leads to abject depression, and the subsequent inability to create. Women on the whole are relatively healthy, having avoided, among other things, the autoanalytic negativism which paralyzes French males!

As I have already indicated, the tendency to judge art from an extra-artistic point of view becomes more pronounced after Ortega's departure for Marburg where, under the tutelage of Cohen and Natorp, it is additionally reinforced by Neo-Kantianism, as well as by an early commitment to socialism.[8] And so it is that between 1907 and 1913, Ortega's censure of his talented modernist contemporaries becomes more pronounced, and is frequently characterized by polemics which are ethnico-political in nature. The case of Azorín, whose work would eventually inspire one of Ortega's definitive critical masterpieces in 1917, by which time he had abandoned Neo-Kantian ethical and political ideals, opting instead for a crucial transition to the radical new methods of phenomenology, is the best case in point, as we shall see in the concluding pages of this introductory chapter.

While there is no significant mention of that great Basque Miguel de Unamuno in Ortega's work prior to his departure for Marburg, there can be no doubt that generous portions of Ortega's early lessons were learned in the pages of the figure who was destined to eclipse him for many years, and who would consistently irritate him after 1906. Ortega's debt to Unamuno, never really fully acknowledged, despite his eulogy to Unamuno on the latter's death and other writings in his praise, can be detected in the earliest of his essays, of which "Maxims," already mentioned with respect to Ortega's censuring of modernist poets, is a good example.

"Maxims" closely resembles the early work of the young socialist Unamuno from almost every point of view: its style, its lexicon, its esthetic ideas - Unamuno was also close to Guyau in this respect -, and its ideas in general, especially those formulated in the section subtitled "New Poetry, Old Poetry," where Ortega belittles esthetic delicacy and where he comes close to reformulating Unamuno's concept of "intrahistory," all recall the iconoclasm of the angry young Basque who was to become the maximal Spanish representative of transcendental, "human" values both in art and in life.[9]

The first public broadside aimed at his former mentor appears in Ortega's work in 1907, in the first article to appear

4

after his departure to Marburg, not long after Unamuno had decided to clamor for the Africanization of Spain. As Ortega no doubt understood, this call to Africanize Spain was a typical Unamunian hyperbole, aimed at a growing number of intellectuals, Ortega among them, who had begun to seek the solution to all of Spain's problems in the magical simplism of Europeanization. Yet Ortega seems to have been inordinately affected by Unamuno's typically indiscreet way of instigating yet another polemic, and in the article in question, he promises his readers a thorough rebuttal of Unamuno's position in the near future, interjecting a gratuitous epithet or two for Unamuno's benefit.[10] These epithets proliferate with each passing year, and, while in 1908, for example, Ortega refers to Unamuno as a turbulent spirit who had exposed Spaniards to many "useless and unhealthy ideas" (118), it is in the article "Unamuno and Europe, a Fable," published in 1909 (128-32), the promised rebuttal, that Ortega's bitterness reaches its climax. In this article, which makes ample use of a letter by the distinguished historian Américo Castro to denigrate Unamuno, Ortega repeatedly refers to Unamuno, to whom Castro was also substantially indebted, as a "possessed Spaniard," and leaves his reader with the general impression that Unamuno's work did more harm than good in Spain. And so it is that the youth who took pride in his aristocratic comportment seems to have lost his composure due to his firm conviction, one which seems to have remained with him for a lifetime, that things European were decidedly preferable to things merely Spanish.

During these same formative years of Ortega's career, in which moral norms were freely used as a basis for judging the literature of his times, his generally negative evaluation of Spanish modernism is extended to include all Spanish culture. Among other places, in his 1911 article "The Art of This World and the Other" (186-205), especially in the section titled "Mediterranean Man," Ortega stereotypes his culture as superficial, vulgar, sordid, to the extent even of citing as an example a certain perverse trivialism which pervades Don Quixote, and to the extent even of misrepresenting Maritornes as "pig Maritornes." Such an assessment of Cervantes' masterpiece in 1911 is truly astonishing, considering the homage paid him just a couple of years later, in 1913, after which date it would become literally impossible for Ortega to even conceive of a "pig Maritornes," due to the fact that he had learned by then to adjust his retina to a more meaningful perspective, just as he implored his audience to adjust theirs in Meditations on the Quixote.

At any rate, "Mediterranean Man," in its narrow representation (or misrepresentation) of Spanish culture, reflects, once again, a set of absolute, rigid cultural norms whose source was the traditional, classical point of view inherited by the Marburg circle. In yet another portion of "The Art of This World and the Other," Ortega contraposes, in compressed form, those rational, ethical, classical norms from which he drew his inspiration during his early period, and which guided his early approach to the modernists: as opposed to the tawdriness of Spaniards, classical man is the supreme paradigm of harmony, order, moderation, correspondence with nature, which he converts into an anthropomorphic world, an image of himself, by rationalizing it. In this way classical man represents the absolute affirmation of life, as opposed to its negation, its dissolution.[11] As M. Arroyo has observed, Ortega's first period is characterized by methodical rationalism, the method most consonant with the view that human life, culture, must be structured in accordance with physico-mathematical, ethical, and esthetic norms.[12] It is not unreasonable to conclude that the early Orteguian ethics, which so colored his esthetic views and his practical criticism, and which played an important role in his attacks against an Unamuno who began displaying an increasing tendency toward a subjective undermining of rationalism, can really be called ethical naturalism.

Pío Baroja, the talented modernist novelist whose cynicism has become legendary, also holds the distinction of being soundly thrashed by Ortega during his pre-phenomenological period, yet another victim of Neo-Kantian cultural norms.

In his first piece on Baroja, "Pío Baroja: The Anatomy of a Disperse Soul" (1910), a portion of which was published posthumously,[13] Ortega leaves his reader with the distinct impression that while he indeed intended to be highly critical of his novelist friend, he also found it necessary to half-apologize for his opinions, intermittently, throughout his essay. This apparent defect, along with certain others, has convinced me that during the composition of the piece in question, Ortega was not entirely sure of himself; that he was not entirely convinced that what he had to say about Baroja in 1910 was really valid. This uncertainty is as surprising as it is atypical.

In addition to such obvious hedging, this first approach to the most popular novelist of his generation impresses me as being the work of a tedious plodder, as opposed to the typical elegance which is the outstanding characteristic of most of the work of this master of prose. Awkward, fastidious, cantankerous, replete with precious metaphor, for which Ortega consistently censures the modernists during this same period, the piece in question contains liberal doses of circular, irrelevant digressions, as well as a generous sprinkling of what is meant to pass as Freudian psychology. With respect to the irritating digressions, it should be made clear that this is not the same type of apparent digression which characterizes much of the circular work

6

of his perspectivist period, where the digression, for the most part, is really related to what Ortega is saying, but rather superfluous, unnecessary in the article in question.

Still, what Ortega does say in his first essay on Baroja is significant, despite its equivocal tone. The following paragraph is perhaps the best example of what it is about Baroja that perturbs Ortega, as well as being a good indication of the values of the young aficionado of things "human."

> One can only lament that for him (Baroja) man begins where the citizen ends, where the anthropoid begins, that organism endowed by vital cosmic energy. I have never read an author who feels greater nostalgia for the orangutan, who so naively believes that man is an orangutan, and nothing more than an orangutan. His work is a complete treatise on the indignity of man (II, 113).

This tendency to proselytize with respect to the absence of human values in Baroja's art is evident throughout Ortega's essay, in which he repeatedly censures his subject's gross cynicism and his ideal of pure "biologism." While conceding that a certain negativism may be necessary as a corrective measure, especially when aimed at Spanish defects, Ortega nevertheless concludes that Baroja, whose attitude is compared to that of the classical canine, takes inordinate delight in negativism for its own sake. In Ortega's eyes, this gratuitous delight is highly suspect, especially since he considers that the primary mission of the novelist is to be socially engaged; to contribute toward the improvement of society through a generally constructive, affirmative attitude rooted in love and virtue. Once again, as was the case especially with Unamuno and Azorín, it can be said that the major thrust of this early commentary by a social idealist is primarily extra-literary, addressed to issues other than Baroja's art as such.

Even in those instances where Ortega does put his finger on certain technical aspects of Baroja's art, and it cannot be denied that "Pío Baroja: Anatomy of a Disperse Soul" represents an early effort toward the identification of an essential structure through lexical signs,[14] he still demonstrates a strong tendency to stray from the matter at hand by extending an innitial observation to an area where he yields to early constructivist temptations. Thus, for example, an initial effort to uncover the substance of Baroja's art through his lexicon culminates in the generalization that Baroja represents a supreme manifestation of a certain national hysteria. While the novelist's pronounced attraction to derisive epithets is equated by Ortega to the "sincerity" that typifies both cynicism and primitive babbling, and while this type of sincerity and good art do not mix, according to Ortega, instead of sticking to his original point (Baroja's language), he next leads us to the abrupt conclusion that primitive babbling is a typical Spanish deficiency. And while ostensibly discussing the picaresque dimension of Baroja's prose, Ortega moves to the conclusion that picaresque art in general is "corrosive," a negative body of literature distinctly wanting with respect to originality, being as it is a mere effort to duplicate reality.

These essentially undeveloped series of impressions and conclusions which characterize Ortega's generally unfavorable view of Baroja would eventually yield, in 1916, to a more coherent, developed, mature, positive view of the best-known Spanish novelist of his time. After having been sufficiently exposed to a more pluralistic approach to things, especially under the tutelage of Scheler, Ortega develops a new appreciation for Baroja's "sincerity," among other things. I shall return to this second approach to Baroja at a more appropriate juncture in this study.

Before moving on to a discussion of Ortega's approach to Azorín, wherein our philosopher offers some of the most conclusive evidence of the huge difference in the way he looked at literature prior to and following his reading of the German phenomenologists, I shall make brief references to certain other pieces from his Marburg period which are of significance from the point of view of what Ortega looked for in a book during these early formative years.

Among the pieces which so qualify are the ones on Antonio Fogazzaro (1908), Maurice Barrès (1910), Ramón Pérez de Ayala (1910), and the great poet Antonio Machado (1912), all included in the first volume of Ortega's works.

Although Ortega finds Fogazzaro's style somewhat frivolous, he praises the Italian novelist for his "extremely noble work," and finds great value in his courageous effort to reform Catholicism, since, according to Ortega, religious sentiment and culture are closely connected (430-38). With respect to Barrès, whose novel he finds "radiant...written in cystal," Ortega's primary interest - Barrès' view of Spain and Franco-German relations - once again eclipses any strict literary interest (468-72). Much the same can be said of Ortega's article on Pérez de Ayala (532-5): while pointing to "minor defects" in his style, Ortega at the same time considers this modernist a "prodigious" writer, yet is more interested in his social message than his art. Ortega fully agrees with the novelist in question that Spanish Jesuits should not be allowed to educate youth because of their tendency to infect students with disdain for the rest of humanity, thus crippling their potential as social leaders. And this same human concern which typifies the early Ortega is also made quite explicit in his article on Antonio Machado (570-74) where he calls for a poetry which is not mere words but which is "inspired by the universe." I shall return to this article on Machado and treat it more extensively in the third chapter of this study.

Besides a brief encomium written in 1913 on behalf of the distinguished modernist Azorín, to which there is appended a letter supporting the writer's candidacy for the Royal Academy,[15] Ortega published four articles on this same figure between 1908 and 1917.

The first two of these articles, "On Petit Philosophy" (1908), and "Beyond Discretion" (1909),[16] while containing minimal references to Azorín as eminent artist, really amount to an ethico-moral evaluation of Azorín the man and his rather serious indiscretions within the political and philosophical arenas. In their own way, these two articles, which tell us nothing about Azorín's art, reflect the attitude of the still impatient, budding young intellectual who had immersed himself in Kant and the Neo-Kantian circle. In his censure of Azorín for practicing unscrupulous journalism with respect to certain political pronouncements, as well as with respect to his effort to discredit certain European thinkers for political motives, Ortega reveals to his reader a strict loyalty to one of the most prevalent normative axioms of the times. Thus, while the reader discerns in the articles in question that Azorín was among Ortega's predilect authors, he is also led to conclude that Ortega's polemic is rooted in the idea of morality as obligation, the rather ideal and abstract moral imperative which was common coin among the Neo-Kantians, later modified by Max Scheler in his critique of formalism in ethics, a critique which in turn was prominent in Ortega's transition to phenomenology.[17]

Ortega's third article on Azorín is titled "A New Book by Azorín" (1912).[18] This article, whose focus is Azorín's Spanish Readings, represents a kind of transitional statement, an approximation of Ortega's final position which postulates that the critic should look at art for what it is, an approximation of that phenomenological, as opposed to the natural posture, of describing through reflection on the thing itself, distinct and separate, disjoined from any a priori values. Yet while Ortega does tell us something substantial about Azorín's art in "A New Book," he is still reluctant to abandon his posture with respect to Azorín's past political charlatanism. In fact, while characterizing Spanish Readings as a perfect book, Ortega naively attributes this perfection to the fact that Azorín somehow acknowledged his guilt regarding his recent fraudulent journalism, and was thus able to purge himself of this guilt ("Katharsis" is the word used by Ortega) as a necessary step toward esthetic perfection. All of which sounds very sophomoric, and not very convincing, especially when we consider that what Ortega is really saying is that the essential elements which he himself isolates as elements that lend unity to Azorín's art did not exist prior to the catharsis which led Azorín to a perfect book, Spanish Readings. Whereupon, Ortega proceeds to demonstrate the contrary, for in his ensuing discussion of Azorín's art in general, he demonstrates quite clearly that these essential elements which characterize Azorín's art did indeed exist in his work prior to his mysterious catharsis, prior to his publication of Spanish Readings.

Nevertheless, what Ortega does say about Azorín's art in "A New Book" is important, for it anticipates how he would eventually look at Azorín in that definitive, critical masterpiece, "The Splendors of the Commonplace," where Ortega himself becomes his own ideal reader - the critic who completes the meaning of a writer's book.

Azorín's artistry, Ortega says in "A New Book," consists of his ability to breach temporality by "suspending the movement of things," by which he means making the past present for his readers. In this way Azorín deprives time of its corrosive power, and forces us to see the past in the present, thus facilitating our ability to project into the future as well.

Yet this is mere "esthetic mechanism," or literary style, Ortega continues. This dimension of Azorín's work would, in and of itself, be inadequate for achieving what we call a book, which can only be achieved by a man who has style, yet who, additionally, locates or "sees" a problem. This talent for seeing a problem "centers us in the universe," according to Ortega.

In the case of Azorín, style is complemented by the ability to appropriate, as his, the problem essential and common to such men as Larra, Costa, Cadalso, as well as to one Cervantes: that huge problem implied in the huge question "Where is Spain?", the question which Ortega himself poses in Meditations. In this way Azorín has tried, according to Ortega, to reconstruct - to make present is what he means - a certain unity of thought centered around a radical problem, a problem common to men living in different times, and to demonstrate to us the evolution of this thought. Thus, Azorín initiates in Spain what Ortega calls "a historical essay of transcendence," by which he means a historical essay which goes much beyond ordinary erudition - much beyond the neat presentation of facts arranged in neat chronological order. In this sense Azorín is a genuine historian.

Notwithstanding the fact that "A New Book" is not as convincing as it was probably meant to be, due principally to the fact that it is sometimes marred by mental lapses and leaps, as well as by incongruency, it is, once again, a significant essay because it marks an early effort on the part of Ortega to isolate the unifying element in the artist's work itself, in Azorín's art as such.

Yet "A New Book" pales in this respect when compared to its companion essay "The Splendors of the Commonplace" (1917),[19] for in this essay, published three years after the publication of Meditations, we encounter a new Ortega, an Ortega in full possession of philosophical tools sharpened by Husserl and Scheler, as well as by his own extraordinary effort in the truncated Meditations. In fact, we can reasonably conclude that one of the intriguing sequels to Meditations, promised (although denied us) in the form of "How Cervantes Was Accustomed to Seeing the World," was actually delayed by some three years and realized in the transposed or substitute form of "How Azorín Was Accustomed to Seeing the World," which we might consider an alternate title for "The Splendors of the Commonplace." In turn, "The Splendors" can be defined, especially in its methodological dimension, as the way in which Ortega finally came around to focusing his enormous eye on the diminutive world of Azorín.

It is important to note that as in the case of Meditations, the setting in "The Splendors" is the Escorial, Ortega's predilect sanctum sanctorum, the epicenter from which he fully relates to things in his world, to his "circumstance." It is this setting which enables him to confront that circumstance in his world known as Azorín's art with raw consciousness, in a state of radical, exclusive, primordial fascination with the object itself, with Azorín's art as such. And this, I think, is the essential meaning of Ortega's transition from Neo-Kantian idealism to the radical neo-realism learned in the works of the early phenomenologists: it means a transition from the world as inviolable nature to its examination as a world of things which I must be personally conscious of, a world in which these things must be loved in a reflexive, as opposed to a geometrical way, as a means toward intuiting their fullest meaning - their "plenitude," to borrow a term used so frequently in Meditations.

Still, the comprehension of the basic methodology which allowed Ortega to realize his intuitive grasp of Azorín's poetics falls short of providing any explanation of the hermeneutic itself, of Ortega's interpretation of the splendid art of Azorín. What is more, the methodology itself poses a formidable problem,

11

for it precludes, by its very circular nature, at least the advisability of any sequential approach to Ortega's essay, which is really a circle of free association from beginning to end, unless we are willing to write several volumes on "The Splendors." While these epic volumes might help us secure an appointment to a major graduate center, they would not necessarily guarantee that we would understand Azorín in Ortega any better than we would if we approach the problem in some other way, perhaps in the way that Ortega might have advised us to approach it. This requires some explanation.

In the presence of the awesome, unorthodox brilliance of pieces such as Meditations, "The Dehumanization of Art," and "The Splendors of the Commonplace," the reader may sense, instinctively perhaps, that he is both witness to, and participant in, a strange drama theretofore rarely, if ever, experienced by him as a reader. If he tries to trace the source of this perplexing feeling (a substantial effort in itself) he would most likely conclude that a certain disjunction is responsible for his rare feeling, a feeling of total abandonment to Ortega's text. What this means, in the case of "The Splendors," is that Ortega succeeds, as was his intention, in blotting out everything extrinsic to the phenomenon itself, to Azorín's "history" itself. In doing so, Ortega not only realizes his own ideal as the demanding spectator, but additionally forces his reader, his spectator, to disjoin himself from the familiar physical world around him, insulating him from any association with his recognizable natural world, thrusting him into a purely mental, one-to-one relationship with what is being described by Ortega. This amounts to the phenomenological ideal of total absorption, and it is in this sense that we as readers can state what we had only vaguely sensed: Ortega is simply contagious.

So then, how shall we separate ourselves from this contagion for the purpose of explaining "The Splendors" in an intelligible way? How do we avoid becoming indefinitely trapped into duplicating Ortega's consciousness of Azorín during his vital act of writing on Azorín, for surely, we simply do not have the time to indulge in such luxury. How do we formulate a reasonably brief, rational, explanatory statement on Azorín as Ortega finally saw him in "The Splendors"? One way is to follow the advice in this matter given by Ortega himself, but only after having read the masterpiece in question several times. We might then step away from it, step back, separate ourselves from its inherent magnetism, establishing some distance between the primary object and our primary awareness of it. In this way, by emulating the painter who witnesses death in "Some Bits of Phenomenology,"[20] we might better equip ourselves to grasp the essential points, the essential outlines of Ortega's essay and therefore substantialize them by translating them into a coherent conclusion. We might then extrapolate the following statement, or something similar to it, with respect to what Azorín means to Ortega in the final analysis:

Azorín is a supreme example of one who senses particular essentials in the past, causes them to relive in the present, and converts them into universal historical essentials, as opposed to the common anecdotal chronology which passes as history. The transition from particular to universal sense is realized because Azorín is a superb stylist who isolates seemingly trivial things and projects, situates these minima within the broader human landscape, thus forcing his reader to view them within their fullest anthropological context, in the context common to all men, in the life-drama common to all men throughout time. All this is what Ortega means when he concludes that Azorín's art "consists of reliving the basic feelings of man throughout the ages."

Now this statement on Ortega's "The Splendors" could be expanded, refined, probably even improved. Yet, provided we do not run away with ourselves, this more refined statement would have a pragmatic meaning quite similar to the meaning of the statement above, which, in methodological terms, underscores the practical, human need to put into abeyance Ortega's consciousness while he was in his dramatic act of writing, in order to extract from his work an intelligible, coherent conclusion.

To summarize these observations on Azorín in Ortega, we can conclude that during the lengthy chronological journey which began with Azorín as sycophantic historian, and which ended with an Azorín who is the maximal Spanish paradigm of genuine historiography, Ortega himself had learned a crucial lesson: the intuition of Mediterranean man is not necessarily, at least not always, wicked and evil.

This evolution in Ortega's way of approaching or "seeing" a book can also be traced chronologically in the way he saw certain other writings, as well as in the way he saw certain painters and painting during and after Marburg.

13

CHAPTER II

PHENOMENOLOGY AND PROSE FICTION

From approximately 1913, the year in which Ortega was busily composing his Meditations, as well as such pioneering pieces as "Sensation, Construction and Intuition," and "On the Concept of Sensation," until he finally abandoned strict criticism in favor of strict ontology, the more intrinsic, morphological approach to literature, directly inspired in phenomenology - an example of which we have seen in Ortega's second approach to Azorín -, became his standard approach. Over the course of more than a dozen years, following the publication of Meditations in 1914, Ortega produced some of the most profound criticism of fiction ever published by European critics, apologizing all the while, in his typical way of drawing attention to himself, for the fact that he was not really a professional literary critic.

This radical originality in the practical criticism produced between 1914 and 1927 is directly related to Ortega's decision to abandon the neat constructive geometry of the Marburg classicists who, Ortega finally decided, were more interested in being right than they were in discovering what was true. What began to crystallize toward 1912, for him as well as for a number of other disenchanted colleagues, was the fact that Neo-Kantian rationalism was suspect, and that the increasing uneasiness and guilt visited on him and his contemporaries had its source in their allegiance to a rather inflexible, doctrinaire philosophic posturing which was, after all was said and done, blatantly inauthentic and even dishonest.

In his autobiographical "Prologue for Germans,"[1] which, in addition to being an attempt to establish his originality, is a treatise on the genesis of phenomenology, after pointing to the shortcomings of the transcendental idealism which was characteristic of the Marburg Kantians, emphasizing the lack of precision in their vocabulary and their proclivity for intellectual gymnastics as opposed to truth, Ortega describes the need to defect from the teachings of his mentors as follows:

> There was no alternative but to row
> toward an imaginary shore. Success was
> improbable. Nevertheless, fortune had
> presented us a prodigious instrument:
> phenomenology. That group of youngsters had
> never been, strictly, Neo-Kantian. Nor did
> it entirely yield to phenomenology. Our will
> toward system prevented that. Phenomenology,
> in its very consistency, is incapable of
> achieving systematic form or shape. Its

> inestimable value lies in the fine structure
> of fleshy tissue which it can offer to the
> architecture of a system. This is why
> phenomenology was not a philosophy for us:
> it was a stroke of good fortune(42).2

Yet the fact of the matter is that Ortega did encounter his new "coastline," where he indeed arrived quite safely, despite this typical tendency to hedge his remarks whenever the subject of crucial influence is involved: by 1913 he had landed precisely in the bosom of "the prodigious instrument of phenomenology," and as M. Arroyo has demonstrated, the landing was a definitive one. Herman Cohen was replaced as chief mentor during this second phase of Ortega's development by Max Scheler, as our Spanish philosopher came to grips with a new pluralism, perspectivism and circumstantiality, all of which were best served by "the prodigious instrument," the radical new methodology advocated by Husserl and disseminated through the pages of the prestigious journal Logos. Even during his final stage of development, where, after reading Heidegger, philosophy becomes ontology, and he is steeped in the systematic pursuit of the meaning of human experience, Ortega's debt to the early phenomenologists remains substantial, as was the case with Heidegger himself, whose ontology was also phenomenological.3

By the end of 1913, Ortega had written two important articles on phenomenology. In the first of these, "Sensation, Construction, Intuition," delivered at the Congress of the Spanish Association for the Advancement of Science,4 Ortega first outlines the current impasse reached both by empiricism and Neo-Kantian constructivism, then proceeds to speak of the "varied and profound" discussions inspired by Husserl's new principle of intuition, ending on the hopeful note that this "presuppositionless" new science might possibly mark the start of a new epoch in philosophy.

The second of these articles on phenomenology, "On the Concept of Sensation,"5 is a critique of a doctoral dissertation by one of Husserl's disciples, Heinrich Hoffman, whose main interest was the application of phenomenology to visual perception. But in addition to being a critique of Hoffman's thesis, Ortega's article, which contains frequent references to Husserl's philosophic milestone, Ideas: A General Introduction to Phenomenology (also published in 1913), is an extremely clear precis of the principles of the "new science" called phenomenology, and in itself constitutes strong evidence that Ortega had converted to phenomenology by the year that Husserl published his widely-acclaimed opus magnus. In his exposition on the essentials of Husserl's new methodology - the role of intuition, consciousness, description, and suspension or bracketing -, we can detect a strong sympathy for the new realism which was in fact to become Ortega's new methodology, and which was to serve him quite generously, notwithstanding any belated objections to Husserl.[6]

The precise influence of Cohen and other Neo-Kantian vestiges to one side, since these have already been adequately documented,[7] Ortega's first book, an incomplete attempt to meditate on Don Quixote, might best be approached as a passionate defense of and call for a new "rigorous science," and, although fractured and frequently vague, one of the earliest European attempts to apply this science to the novel.

It is generally acknowledged that Meditations on the Quixote is one of the most difficult books ever published in the Castilian language. Among other reasons, this difficulty is due in large measure to the absence of any clear connection between the various parts of the book. This is true not only of the relationship of the three basic divisions of the book to one another, but true also of the relationship of the various and multiple ideas expressed within the sections of each basic division. Thus the reader of Meditations is at first glance confronted by a rather frustrating elusiveness, a kind of oblique, elliptical, circular maneuvering which seems construed for the express purpose of denying reasonable access to what one simultaneously senses, almost instinctively, to be the profound thoughts and conclusions of an unusual philosopher. Even the most patient of readers may be tempted to conclude that he has been left directionless, abandoned to the whims of a supremely metaphorical somnambulist who might have practiced surrealism instead of philosophy.

I shall resort to a kind of synoptic parapharasing of the first few pages (four sections) of Ortega's "Preliminary Meditation," the second chapter of Meditations, in an effort to reconstruct a fair approximation of the typical reader's initial reaction to these apparently transitionless, fractured meditations.

In the few pages in question, Ortega first fixes our senses on the countryside adjacent to the Escorial Monastery, forcing them to indulge in a splendid array of color and sound: coppers, yellows, greens, emeralds and purples, all steeped in a silence never quite absolute, compete with murmuring brooks and the subtle melodies of greenfinches, orioles, linnets, nightingales.

Next we are asked to see the forest as both surface and depth; from surfaces and depths we are led to the hidden dimension of a spherical body such as an orange, and back again to the forest and its streams and orioles, its oak roots and

17

other phenomena. From this world of impressions we are led to worlds beyond, or to "higher realities," and to a summary conclusion that the ultimate dimension of the countryside is God - in Platonic terms an idea, similar to the idea which is the third dimension of an orange.

As the reader attempts to chart a course through this very lyric, rapid, disjointed enigma, he will, more likely than not, be tempted to question both the legitimacy of Ortega's meditations and their relationship to a book titled Don Quixote. Above all, what is the apparent connection between purple flowers, splendid nightingales, enchanting brooks, an oak, an orange, and the great novel authored by one humble Miguel de Cervantes?

Nevertheless, despite the disconcerting stylistic and structural aspects of Meditations, Ortega's book does make sense, both as strict philosophy and as a new direction in literary criticism.

The fact of the matter is, although cryptic in nature, Ortega's preface to Meditations, which he titles "To the Reader," is a kind of exegetic appendix of directions for the reader conditioned to traditional approaches to literary criticism. While Ortega himself has provided in his preface clear evidence that the elliptical nature of his meditations is intentional,[8] and while these directions are in themselves somewhat vague, requiring of the reader that he adjust to a kind of thought by association process, the directions are nevertheless available. My effort to reformulate, or systematize these directions, as well as my interpretation of the rest of Meditations, are, of course, subject to error, in which case I bear sole responsibility.

A substantial portion of Ortega's preface, in which he tells us that his book was inspired by "amor intellectualis," is devoted to the concept of love and its relationship to the objects which surround us. This relationship can be systematized as follows: all the mute things which surround us, our circum-stantia, the objects which life places in our path, "like the remains of a shipwreck," including the most insignificant of objects, contain within themselves the possibility of "plenitude" or perfection. To achieve their maximal fruition, these objects require that we fully love them, that we become fully conscious of their capacity for plenitude, that we link ourselves to them by fixing our loving attention on them, instead of walking among them blindly, as we have been conditioned to do, unaware of their potential.[9] Since it is love which binds us to all things, love is "an extension of the individuality which absorbs other things into it, which unites them to us." It is this union which allows us to acquire a more profound understanding of the properties of the objects which surround us. In short, when Ortega asks that we love all things, he is asking us, additionally, to fix our sights on things in a new way, to make the optical adjustment required for seeing essences beneath surfaces.

Love is essential to understanding. Among the various aspects of love, we may include the urge to comprehend, and it is for this reason perhaps, according to Ortega, that Plato referred to the need to understand as "the madness of love." The need to understand is also compared by Ortega to a religion, or to a religious obsession of sorts.

Inasmuch as philosophy is a science of synthesis, which equips us with the potential to understand both greater and lesser things and their relationship to one another, Ortega considers that philosophy is "the general science of love," and concludes that we must distinguish between this science of love and mere erudition, or the accumulation of facts. True understanding, as opposed to knowledge, is true illumination, and is comparable to "a sudden discharge of intellectual insight."[10] Even when particular doctrines are eventually proved erroneous, philosophy receives a new life from these ruins in the form of a renewed urge toward understanding, toward further illumination we might say.

A phenomenon similar to this illumination is operative in the dynamic process through which we acquire culture. What we call culture is simply our circum-stantia in distilled, purified form; the objects which surround us in raw form, "the spontaneous" or "immediate," contracted or transfigured into something socially meaningful. In order to achieve this meaning, we must extract from the things that are our circumstance, from the things which compose the world around us, their inner logos. This in turn requires the active participation of the individual, his creative act, as well as a certain distance between him and the phenomenon observed in his immediate surroundings.

Love, then, one's individual circumstance, philosophy, culture, the creative act, are inseparable and are in turn associated by Ortega with "perspective," which in his introduction to the reader of Meditations he refers to as "the ultimate reality." And one's perspective, he continues, is perfected by the precision with which we react to the various levels which make up the multiple viewpoints of said perspective. Perspective is further described and linked to circumstance as follows:

> Fine; a perspective is perfected by the
> multiplication of its terms and the precision

with which we react to each of its levels.
The intuition of higher values fertilizes our
contact with the minimal ones, and love for
what is close and small makes the sublime
real and manifest in our hearts. For the one
for whom small things are nothing, neither
does the great exist.

We must seek our circumstance, such as
it may be, precisely in its limitation, in
its peculiarity, its proper place in the
enormous perspective of the world. We ought
not be detained perpetually in ecstasy in the
face of hieratic values, but rather conquer
for our individual life the proper place
among them. In sum: the reabsorption of
circumstance is the concrete destiny of man
(321-2).

Immediately following the passage quoted above, Ortega
describes his own personal circumstance, culminating in his
famous statement "I am myself and my circumstance." What he
tells us explicitly about himself and his circumstance is that
the other half of his person is formed by a sector of the
Guadarrama range which is his "circumstantial reality," his
"natural exit toward the universe." Ortega explains that only
through this sector can he integrate himself and be fully
himself. The reader should understand that he is referring to
the area where the Escorial is located, much frequented by Ortega
in his youth, the setting for his "Preliminary Meditation," as it
was for his inquiry into Azorín.

What he tells us about self and circumstance in a more
indirect way is that to be fully conscious of one's circumstance
implies intentionality, or the reciprocal implication of self and
world, what Magliola, in his study on phenomenology and
literature refers to as "the epistemology of mutual
implication."[11] This reciprocal implication of subject and
object is alluded to through an example from biology, in which
Ortega explains that biological science approaches a living
organism as a compendium of body and environment. He concludes
that the life process consists both of adaptation of organism to
environment and adaptation of environment to organism.

This example, through which Ortega attempts to reinforce the
concept of the mutual interdependence of subject and object, is
then supplemented by a fleeting reference to phenomenological
precepts: in order to save the self, Ortega says, one must save
one's circumstance, or save "the appearances, the phenomena,"

which is to say that one must "look for the meaning of what surrounds us."

The few concluding pages of Ortega's introduction deal with literary criticism and Don Quixote per se. Criticism, like philosophy, is also viewed as a labor of love by Ortega. The function of criticism, he says, is not to appraise or judge literary works - as he himself had been doing consistently up to this point -, but rather to complete them through love, thus bringing out "the full potential of a chosen work." Above all, this means that criticism must have an affirmative purpose. It must provide all the aids necessary for the reader to experience the most intense and clearest impression possible, "to endow the reader with a more perfect visual organ so that the work is completed by reading it."[12]

All this is the opposite of what someone like St. Beuve does, according to Ortega. The French critic is mentioned as a good example of what criticism is not, or should not be, since all Sainte-Beuve succeeds in doing is to take us to and fro, from work to author, stuffing his criticism with insignificant anecdotes.[13]

With respect to Ortega's own critical approach to Don Quixote, his stated purpose is a study of "Quixotism." However, what quixotism means for Ortega and what it means for others are two different things. As opposed to the quixotism of Don Quixote himself, Ortega tells us that he intends to study the quixotism of the book. By this he means that he intends to avoid the common, serious errors which are the result of an isolated treatment of Don Quixote's character. These errors usually translate into one of two extreme points of view, incomplete and invalid, since Cervantes himself meant to carry his reader beyond the traditional conflict between realism and idealism:

> Nevertheless, the errors to which the isolated treatment of Don Quixote has led are truly grotesque. Some, with charming foresight, propose that we not be Quixotes; others, in accordance with the latest fashion, invite us to an absurd existence, full of extravagant gestures. For the some and the others, apparently, Cervantes did not exist. Well, Cervantes came upon this earth to carry our spirit beyond this dualism (326).[14]

Since we can only understand an individual through his kind, Ortega continues, it would be wise to consider that "the individual Don Quixote is an individual of the species

21

Cervantes," and that this is so because as opposed to physical things, "the artistic thing" - like the character of Don Quixote - "is made of a substance called style." The esthetic object, therefore, can be defined as "the individualization of a protoplasm-style."

When we consider, then, that Don Quixote represents only a partial manifestation of Cervantine style, the wise critic should try to avoid focusing his attention exclusively on the protagonist, and opt instead to examine the whole of Cervantes' book, its "vast surface," in order to achieve a clearer, more complete notion of Cervantine style:

> It suits us, then, to make the effort to divert our sight from Don Quixote, focusing it on the rest of the work, so as to extract from its vast surface the broadest and clearest concept of Cervantine style, of which the noble Manchegan is only a particular condensation. For me this is the true Quixotism: the Quixotism of Cervantes, not of Don Quixote. And not in the Cervantes imprisoned in Algiers, not in his life, but in his book. In order to escape this biographical and erudite detour, I prefer the title Quixotism to Cervantism (327).

This task, the examination of quixotism, Ortega readily admits, in the concluding portion of his introduction, is an enormous one, so difficult indeed that the author of Meditations senses that he will not fully succeed in wresting the secrets of Cervantine style. Nevertheless, his decision to examine the "vast surface" of Don Quixote is irrevocable, for he is "fatally attracted to the immortal work," although his intuition about not completing the enormous task proved true in the end.

What one needs, if he is to undertake the enormous responsibility which the proper examination of Don Quixote implies, is enormous patience, "laborious attention," for an artistic masterpiece only yields, if it yields at all, to the "meditative cult." One must, according to Ortega, take Don Quixote as Jericho was taken: "In wide circles, our thoughts and emotions pressing on it slowly, resounding in the air like ideal trumpets" (327). So it is that Ortega describes his own meditations on Cervantes' masterpiece as "wide circles of attention which our thought traces without haste, at a distance," an obvious reference to the predilect phenomenological hermeneutic.[15]

In the conclusion to his introduction, Ortega informs his reader that his meditations were largely inspired by a patriotic preoccupation. One of his main purposes is what he refers to as "a rejection of a decadent Spain," and the communication of this rejection to other kindred souls who have rejected her. Yet this rejection of a stagnant Spain, the myopic Spain which so often plagued Ortega during the entire course of his career,[16] bears with it the obligation to pave the way toward another Spain. It is for this reason that Ortega concludes his introduction with the observation that the most intimate and personal of his meditations amount to "experiments on a new Spain."

With these rather loosely associated directions for reading from Ortega's introduction in mind, the reader is probably prepared to chart a more meaningful course through the remainder of Meditations, and begin to make more sense of the "wide circles of attention." In fact, the first few pages of the meditation addressed to the reader, which I have summarized closely above, can themselves be viewed as a circle whose full course may be said to run from the phenomena in the forest to Don Quixote and Spain somewhat as follows: the splendid colors, sounds, trees, etc. are the phenomenal elements - surfaces, impressions - which, taken together, form that depth or possibility which we call a forest. In order to fully intuit and appreciate this depth, this possibility which is "the latent as such," we must discard the passive type of vision which is satisfied with surfaces and learn instead to see that dimension of inwardness of the phenomena which make up the forest. This requires that the spectator establish a certain distance between himself and the phenomenon viewed, and that, in addition, he will or desire (intend) the inwardness, depth, concealed dimension.

The introductory paragraph to the fifth section of the "Preliminary Meditation," which is titled "Restoration and Erudition," provides us with a clearer connection between surfaces, depth, "foreshortening" - in the sense of contracting or abridging depth -, and Don Quixote and Spain as follows:

> The forest opens up its depths around me. I have a book in my hand: Don Quixote, an ideal forest.

> Here is another instance of depth: that of a book, the depth of this maximal book. Don Quixote is the foreshortened book par excellence.

> There was an epoch in Spanish life when no one wanted to recognize the depth of the Quixote. This period of history came to be

23

known as the Restoration. During that period
the heart of Spain slowed to the least number
of beats per minute (337).

This is tantamount to saying that during the Spanish
Restoration (1874-1923) Quixote criticism was notoriously
inadequate, and that it was inadequate precisely because of its
refusal to see the forest for the trees, because of its refusal
to look beyond the immediately phenomenal, the immediately
apparent, the immediate surface or impression. The ideal forest,
that extra-phenomenal or phenomenological depth which is Don
Quixote, was completely ignored.

The greater portion of the remaining ten chapters of the
"Preliminary Meditation" is addressed to an explanation of this
Spanish refusal to see depth. From the specific inadequacy of
the Restoration, Ortega proceeds throughout these remaining
chapters, typically, to what he considers to be the inadequacy of
Spanish thought in general, and relates this general inadequacy
to the general "sensism" of Mediterranean culture, as he was
often prone to doing. By "sensism" Ortega here means the general
inability, or refusal, to see past mere impressions, and the
concomitant association of impressions with realism. The fact of
the matter is that as opposed to Greek art, which always aspired
toward the typical and essential beneath concrete appearances,
Latin art, for some twenty centuries, has always been
characterized by its determination to imitate reality.[17] The
Mediterranean, according to Ortega, instead of seeking the
essence of an object, seeks "its presence, its actuality," or
"the harsh fierceness of the actual as such." This almost
exclusive reliance on the senses implies, in turn, a deficiency
in analysis, and it is characteristic of the Mediterranean in
general, and the Spaniard specifically, that they are deficient
with respect to thinking, conceptualizing. It is strongly
inferred that they are in dire need of a rigorous new science.[18]

Yet at the same time it is significant that while Ortega
rejects exclusive reliance on sensualism, he does not propose
that the Spaniard abandon his clear vision of the external world,
but rather defends it, for the first time, to my knowledge, and
urges that the Spaniard integrate his energetic impressionism
with that other tradition which is required for the realization
of depth. Indeed, how would a converted practitioner of
consciousness practice his new science without the benefit of
keen eyes? In chapter thirteen of the preliminary meditation
("Integration"), Ortega has the following to say:

On the moral map of Europe we represent
the predominance of the impression. The
concept has never been our element. There is

no doubt that we would be unfaithful to our destiny were we to abandon the energetic affirmation of impressionism latent in our past. I do not propose abandonment, but the contrary: an integration.

> Pure tradition cannot mean...anything but a terra firma for the support of individual discrepancies. Our culture can never be this if it does not affirm and center its sensualism within the cultivation of meditation(359).

All of which amounts to a clear call for the new methodology which was to become the definitive one in the post-Meditations Ortega.

The concluding chapter of Ortega's preliminary meditation ("Criticism as Patriotism"), which addresses the problem of Spain, Spanish tradition, and Don Quixote, completes yet another wide circle. In the chapter in question, Ortega rejects the notion that Spain must follow some sort of national tradition, for this route can only lead to disaster, as it had so often in the past. He proposes that Spain burn her past, her "inert traditional mask," in a bonfire. To be patriotic, it is strongly implied, is to liberate oneself from the stagnant past in quest of a new Spain, Spain as a possibility, as a supreme promise, unfulfilled, with the exception of some half-dozen high water marks. One of these half-dozen places in which Spain throbs with intensity is the work of Cervantes, "a Spanish plenitude."

> One of these essential experiences, perhaps the greatest, is Cervantes. This is a Spanish plenitude. This is a word which we can always brandish like a sword. If we only knew with certainty what constitutes the style of Cervantes, the Cervantine way of approaching things, we would achieve everything. Because at these spiritual heights there reigns an inviolable unity and a poetic style bears within itself a philosophy, morality, a science, and a politics. If some day someone would come along and discover the profile of Cervantine style, it would suffice for us to extend its lines to the rest of our collective problems so that we might awaken to a new life. Then, if there exists among us courage and genius, we could initiate a new Spanish effort in its purest form (363).

At this juncture it might prove useful to extend our extrapolation of the introduction to the preliminary meditation to read somewhat as follows: the vast, unlimited surface which is Cervantes' masterpiece, a Spanish circumstance, an ideal forest, a perspective, conceals a depth, a possibility, a plenitude, an unusual promise which ought to be dis-covered or illuminated through patience and love, through meditation and amor intellectualis. Such dis-covery of plenitude would necessitate an active (reflexive), as opposed to a passive (impressionistic) way of seeing things, in addition to the will to dis-cover, to illuminate the forest beyond its trees, the latent as such. He who would, in short, undertake the awesome burden of approaching Don Quixote in a fresh, phenomenological way, spurning strictly phenomenal or natural approaches, would be the genuine patriot-hero who might pave the way toward a new Spain, toward a new habit of seeing things in a primordial, as opposed to a traditional way.

Ortega himself tried to become that patriot who would guide Spain to a new way of seeing things through an example of what he projected as a model in practical criticism, beginning with his "First Meditation," the third and final part of the book which, unfortunately, he never finished. This first meditation, appropriately subtitled "A Short Treatise On the Novel," might also have been titled "What a Novel Is and Is Not." The portion in question can be viewed as a wide circle of attention containing within it many smaller circles addressed to esthetics, culminating in the thesis that a novel is a tragicomic genre. The pages under discussion are addressed more directly to the novel in general, as well as to Don Quixote in particular. They were obviously meant as a prolegomenon to what would have been a scrupulously structured phenomenology of stylistics, whose express purpose would have been the dis-covery, the unlocking of the essential form of Cervantes' style.

The journey which culminates in the thesis that the novel is tragicomedy begins with the simple question "What is a novel"?, and only comes to an end after the reader of the first (and last) meditation is treated to a series of fresh approaches to literary genre, the epic, myth, the chivalric romance, poetry and reality, mime, lyricism, comedy and tragedy, among other things. The brief, sparkling reflections devoted to these various concepts are provocative, and can be viewed as the practical manifestation of what Ortega means by probing beneath surfaces, delving into depths, using active vision, dis-covering essences. One can only conclude that it was supreme attention, supreme consciousness of the object of attention, supreme perception integrated with the concept - supreme "love" - which were responsible for the originality of the conclusions reached in the chapters in question.

In any case, the fact that our circular journey begins with the simple question "What is a novel"?, a question which people who wrote on novels at that time rarely thought about, is a significant one, for the questioning of what had been accepted as something obvious sets the tone for the entire meditation in question. Ortega's opening paragraph is calculated to demonstrate to the reader the wisdom of beginning his approach to Cervantes in the most elemental way, in an effort to remove any doubt regarding the determination that his meditation on the novel will be a presuppositionless one, unobscured by any received meaning which might intrude on this exercise in free love and its pristine reflection on the thing itself. By beginning on ground level, by setting to one side just about everything ever said about the novel, as well as rejecting the accepted wisdom on this and related matters, Ortega is here paving the way for the application of a methodology analogous to Husserl's phenomenological reduction, an exercise in "ideation" or the intuition of essences whose point of departure is the original outer perception, and which culminates, ideally, in a new concept, which in turn can be considered a new object. This is the basic methodology of the rigorous new science. With respect to its application to the novel, its fundamental requirement would entail a reflective description of our experience with the novel in strict accordance with its own essential nature, with the essential nature of the novel as such, as opposed, let us say, to our perception of the novel as this was inherited through a Sainte-Beuve, a Juan Valera, a Menéndez Pelayo.[19]

And this is precisely what Ortega has done throughout his final meditation, separating or "disconnecting" himself from the natural standpoint in order to exploit the basic method of ideation.

I shall use the concrete example of the very brief (three paragraph) section titled "The Windmills," which I might take the liberty of subtitling "A Phenomenology of Culture," as a good case in point. In this inquiry into the quixotic perception of windmills as giants, Ortega "transvalues" the concept of giants, objects which exist in culture, through an intuition of their essence, and then transfers this "transvaluation," which we can call a new concept, to the general realm of culture, in an effort to "illuminate," to shed fresh light on its essential meaning.

Typically, in this case, the physical description of the phenomena involved, as these present themselves in nature to our consciousness, precedes any theoretical extrapolation with respect to their own nature.

While accompanying Don Quixote and Sancho in their meandering through the Montiel countryside, Ortega explains, he became aware of the true aspect of all things, their raw physical presence, their "absolute substance," what they are prior to and beyond the meaning derived from their interpretation, and what they become subsequent to their interpretation, which, ideally, should be their essential intuition.

In Montiel, a horizon of brilliant sunsets, "injected with blood," there rise up to the heavens flour mills, which are a marvel to behold. These mills in the sunset, like all things, have a meaning, and this meaning is that they are giants. Now the fact that Don Quixote may indeed be unbalanced does not provide an explanation for this meaning, for the fact of the matter is, according to Ortega, that our knight, who insists on giants, is merely practicing what is and will always be "normal" for the rest of humanity.

Although Don Quixote's giants may be an illusion, how is this illusion born? What about "giants in general" - by which Ortega means, I shall add, the giants existing throughout time in all cultures and understood by all men, giants as a cultural reality -, and what about the occasion on which man first conceived this Cervantine giant? Well, it must have been a similar occasion, for:

> In the girating wings there exists a suggestion of colossal arms. If we obey the impulse of this allusion and allow ourselves to be taken along the curve articulated there, we shall arrive at the giant (385).

Now we are prepared to pinpoint the exact moment in which Ortega's consciousness of mills and giants leads him to a climactic revelation, to a new concept, to the "dis-covery" of the essence of a universal phenomenon understood by all men throughout time: this moment of intuition occurs precisely when Ortega obeys his natural impulse to extend the incomplete curve, thus completing the meaning of a giant by retracing its genesis, by unraveling it before our eyes in status nascens. This we can call perceptual genetic phenomenology.[20]

In the final paragraph of "The Windmills," Ortega extends his conclusion on the genesis of giants as cultural phenomena to a theory on the birth of culture in general. This theory can be freely summarized as follows: what we call culture stems originally from the idealization of something material in our

28

environment. This idealization entails a kind of mirage, illusion, poetry, creativity which gives birth to a new concept, a new cultural object. This would include such abstract concepts as justice, truth, as well as other spiritual cultural values.

As I have already mentioned, in the final chapter of Meditations, Ortega pursues the question "What is a novel?" to the conclusion that a novel is tragicomedy. The central concepts through which he arrives at this conclusion include reality and the heroic, the tragic and the comic, and the relationship of each of these to one another. Before proceeding to the concluding, summary section of the meditation in question, I shall briefly systematize the relationship between these concepts as follows: reality is to the comic what the heroic (including the will) is to the tragic. In addition, there exists an inverse relationship between these elements, so that reality represents the negation of the heroic, just as the comic represents the negation of the tragic. And it is precisely the tension or clash between the reality of the comic spirit - "mere deposit, inertia" - and the visionary poetry of the tragic idealist who would transform the established order ("mere presence"), that forms that third dimension of the novel which is its essential "esthetic depth." Don Quixote, being as it is the most salient example of such esthetic depth, is the greatest of all novels.

"Flaubert, Cervantes, Darwin," the final section of Meditations, can be viewed as a kind of synthetic statement which attempts to generalize the relationship between the tragiheroic, Cervantine (Orteguian) world view, largely implicit in the conclusions drawn throughout the section in question, and the contrary world view as manifested in the nineteenth century, which we may also refer to as the Darwinian, postivist, realist, or naturalistic world view. Owing to Ortega's customary reluctance to elaborate fully on many of his concluding statements in the normal expository manner, understandable because he is not writing normal exposition, the significance of these statements is in many cases considerably more extensive than is immediately apparent. For reasons relating to Ortega's insistence that the reader of Meditations cultivate the comprehensive alertness required for extracting the fullest possible meaning from his synthetic conclusions, his insistence that the reader bent on absorbing the broadest meaning from his synthetic conclusions must have first absorbed all the obliquely-related prior conclusions set forth in the circular Meditations, Ortega's reader is forced into the complementary role of supplying for himself what is frequently only alluded to. In my discussion of the final pages of Meditations therefore, I shall take the liberty of reasonably extending the meaning of certain of his summary statements in an effort to clarify some of the broader implications of these same statements.

Following some introductory comment regarding the presence of Don Quixote in all novels,[21] in addition to some speculation regarding the diminishing appeal of the contemporary novel as compared to our continuing enthusiasm for Cervantes' masterpiece,[22] Ortega isolates his predilect bête noire, realism, and concludes that the nineteenth century paid exclusive homage to "facts," deifying reality as its ideal. He next states that we are the offspring of a century characterized by bitterness, "a perverse delight in pessimism," and that as a result our present century has been contaminated by animosity.

While never quite stating it explicitly, Ortega allows us to infer, mainly through sequential association, that our immediate predecessor, the nineteenth century, took it upon itself, in a negative, vindictive, destructive way, to cleanse the universe of all its nefarious, hallucinatory heroism; to crush its subversive idealists by forcing them to behave in accordance with the implacable tenets of real presence, in the name of material progress. We can also extrapolate from what Ortega implies that according to him - and this is but a prelude to both "The Dehumanization of Art" and The Rebellion of the Masses- nineteenth century realism was the single most deadly enemy of all that is innovative, cultural, lofty, new. Realism, in short, like its counterpart, bourgeois democracy, is a great conservative leveler, championed, of course, by the myopic mass.

In the ensuing paragraph, the author of Meditations examines the contribution of the natural sciences to the eradication of originality and the banishment of freedom. Darwin is a fundamental culprit, for scientific determinism and adaptation are equated to submission, renunciation, the absence of originality and freedom. Under circumstances dictated by the environment, heroes vanish from the face of the earth as man becomes matter, as his actions become reactions. We can summarize the paragraph in question by stating that, according to Ortega, a man without a will is a vegetable, or mere inert "thereness."

When social and biological determinism are imposed on the structuring of the novel, the result is, of course, a phenomenon like Emile Zola. And the concluding passages of Meditations dwell on this transfer of scientific determinism to the novel in rather apocalyptic terms: Zola is to the history of the novel what Darwin is to the history of thought is a fair approximation of what Ortega implies. The naturalism of the French novelist represents, according to Ortega, the apotheosis of the environment to the extent that the individual protagonist, no longer responsible for his acts, disappears from the pages of the novel, a victim of its environment, its milieu. Concomitantly, in the name of verisimilitude, physiology, physics and positivism, art, poetry, the tragic, and the beautiful in general, are thoroughly purged from fiction.

We can now take the liberty of reading into, or "completing" the meaning of these compressed generalizations on Darwin and Zola as follows: as compared to the Cervantine plenitude, the ideal forest, the vast provocative surface, the unlimited possibility, the esthetic depth and plenitude which is Don Quixote, the myopic realism of the nineteenth century novel, particularly the naive realism of Zola, with its monodimensional scope, restricted to the present as such, represents the sterile kind of "sensism" (impressionism, apparentism) typical of Mediterranean and all mass cultures. Zola's extrinsic, phenomenal world, which communicates the impression of things as opposed to the things themselves, represents a passive, as opposed to an active (visuo-conceptual) way of seeing things. This lack of love for things in turn precludes the possibility of illumination, dis-covery, truth, and implies a deficiency of inner powers - both on the part of the Zola aficionado as well as on the part of Zola himself, I think Ortega would agree.

We can further extend the Orteguian statements in question to include the meaning that Zola's sensualism, together with the absence of the bold adventurer who would dislocate the established material order, who would reform or radicalize reality, presupposes a parallel absence of the poetic tension necessary for the success of that tragicomic genre known as the novel, for Zola's fiction precludes that Cervantine third dimension, the esthetic depth born of the conflict between heroic will and reality. Thus it is that the poetic reality which characterized Cervantes' novel is replaced in Zola's work by what we can now refer to as inert presence, mere deposit, the here and the now. All of which, of course, makes for some very dull reading, or the kind of reading generally favored by the dull masses.

Between the publication of Meditations and an essay on Gabriel Miró (1927), Ortega continued to practice criticism of fiction sporadically, either in a form whose main focus was a single literary figure, or in the form of a commentary included as a part of other pieces whose primary focus was not fiction. All these pieces provide eloquent testimony that his fundamental methodological approach to the novel was phenomenological.

Besides "The Splendors of the Commonplace," which I have treated in the first chapter of this study, Ortega published, during the period under consideration, separate pieces on Baroja, Proust, Dostoyevsky, Stendhal, Anatole France, as well as on less-known figures, while he included, as well, in his briefer comments, significant references to the work of figures such as Balzac and Flaubert, among others.

I shall first consider the problem of what can properly be called a psycho-esthetic reflection on Ortega's post-Kantian Baroja, his 1916 essay titled "Ideas On Pío Baroja,"23 a significant modification of his earlier piece on the same author, which, like the magnificent piece on Azorín published in the following year, is one more example of _amor intellectualis_ applied to fiction - yet another example of small circles of attention (meditations, also) within a wider circle, all calculated so as to compel us as readers to see a new Baroja, the essential and complete Baroja as he becomes unraveled in the reflective consciousness of Ortega.

Having overcome the idea that culture is traditional logic, ethics, and esthetics, and having had the experience and advantage, as he had in the case of Azorín, of attempting to apply the new science to _Meditations_, notwithstanding the Neo-Kantian vestiges of this work, Ortega was, by 1916, fully prepared to delve into the prolific Baroja in a much more meaningful way than he did in his earlier attempt, discussed in the first chapter of this study.

In its broader sense, "Ideas On Baroja" can be considered the first decisive evidence of Ortega's renunciation or definitive abandonment of the type of ideological criticism wherein the literary text was subordinate to some higher truth, a pretext for the extra-critical search for the human values which especially characterized the criticism of his first period. This time, far from criticizing Baroja for his inhuman and antisocial negativism, as he had done in his first attempt to approach the cynic, "the canine," Ortega now finds this posture a positive virtue, and even defends it. Baroja's man as orangutan no longer alarms the Spanish philosopher, and the picaresque literature of peripheral vagabonds is no longer corrosive. Baroja's sincerity - his scathing language and his abrasive rejection of the established order of things, in which perhaps Ortega now sensed some parallel with his own rejection of the traditional order of things - is no longer in and of itself a counterproductive element in his art. As a matter of fact, in his defense of Baroja's nihilism, Ortega, normally the implacable enemy of all forms of romanticism, at times sounds very much like a romantic, finding in the novelist's iconoclasm a certain spiritual dynamism, a certain robust individualism which is sadly lacking in a community which needs to be cured of its stagnant utilitarianism, its servility to the commonplace, its complacency.

From among the multiple circles which make up "Ideas On Baroja," we can isolate three fundamental reflections and define them as follows: a reflection or treatise on literary criticism; a core psychological reflection in the form of an inquiry into the most frequently-recurring pattern in the works of Baroja; a reflection, in the form of a definitive judgment, on Baroja's art as such. With respect to his art as such, Baroja is lacking, as we shall see.

While he mentions neither Husserl nor phenomenology, Ortega's meditation on literary criticism, a theoretical prologue to its actual application to Baroja, really amounts to an obvious defense of the critical approach later adopted by the Geneva School, the so-called critics of consciousness, the best-known practitioners of phenomenological criticism.[24] The basic tenets of phenomenological literary analysis all appear in extremely condensed form in the second and sixth chapters of Ortega's essay, titled respectively "Theme and Style," and, significantly enough, "Esthetic Intention and Literary Criticism."

The reading of literature as the embodiment of the consciousness of an author, the intentionality of this unique consciousness, the idea that literary style and the work itself originate in these intentional acts of consciousness, the collaborative or "co-creative" role of the critic in isolating and identifying these objects of consciousness as keys to the author's complete works, among other phenomenological tenets, are all set forth by Ortega in a single paragraph of the second chapter of "Ideas On Baroja."

After a terse reminder that reading is always "a collaboration" - something that Unamuno had insisted on time and again in his works -, Ortega informs us that a writer's style, or "the physiognomy of his work," consists of "a series of selective acts executed by him." From among the infinite things at his disposal, the innumerable things, including words, which form the unlimited possibility which is the world around him - shades of Husserl again - the writer, Ortega explains, will choose to focus on an object which he converts into the "general object" or central theme of his work. The job of the critic, Ortega concludes, is to isolate this generic object, the element around which the author orients his production:

> And we see how the writer, from among
> all those innumerable things, chooses one and
> makes it the core theme of his work. Style
> begins with this primary selection: it is
> decisive. As the growing plant, compelled by
> some mysterious appetite, leans or contorts
> in its quest for light, so does the writer's

spirit orient itself toward its object, confronting it, leaving all other things to one or another side. There exists a prior, latent affinity between an artist's most intimate self and a specific portion of the universe. This choice, which ordinarily is not a deliberate one, stems, of course, from the poet's conviction that this object is the best instrument for expressing the esthetic theme that he bears within him, that facet of the world which best reflects his intimate emanations. For this reason, literary criticism has, in my opinion, to begin by isolating this generic object, which is the element around which the whole work is oriented (70).

These ideas on the role of criticism with respect to the intentionality of consciousness, with respect to the isolation of latent experiential patterns, culminate in the sixth chapter of Ortega's essay on Baroja, "Esthetic Intention and Literary Criticism," essentially a defense of immanent literary criticism. After informing us that we can only judge Baroja after having searched his work for what he wanted to put into it, after discovering "his will and intention," - after first understanding him properly - Ortega offers, typically, an example from painting as the proper way of "seeing" art, as opposed to the typical citizen's way of looking at it. The example used is El Greco, and the realist who looks at his painting one who is predisposed to discovering similarities between the painted surface and a slice of existing corporeality. Now since El Greco, for the most part, never really intended to paint such similarities, the realist in question can only find him perplexing, as the incongruence between his predisposition and the canvas itself leaves him with a sense of failure. Quite like the vulgar masses in "The Dehumanization of Art," the realist who does not know how to focus his eye concludes that the artist is to blame. The meaning of the example summarized above, never quite spelled out by Ortega, is, of course, that the naive realist conditioned to looking at art from the natural standpoint, unable to adjust his retina in accordance with the precepts of the new science, can never become a good phenomenologist, and, consequently, can never become a decent critic.

The section in question ends with the summary statement by Ortega that the only legitimate goal of literary criticism should be to teach one how to read books by "adjusting the reader's eyes to the author's intention."

A logical question now follows: Just how does Ortega himself isolate the latent pattern which pervades Baroja's works, the key both to the essence of his art and, in this case, his psychology? How does Ortega adjust our eyes to Baroja's intention? How does he arrive at the climactic assessment of Baroja's "eidos" that appears in the concluding pages of his essay, aptly titled "Prose and the Man"?

One way we can begin to address these questions is by agreeing to follow Ortega's own advice, trying first to trace some sort of recurring referential pattern in Ortega's assessment of Baroja's consciousness, for such a pattern, intercalated throughout Ortega's essay, does indeed exist.

Beginning with a preliminary reference to Baroja as "a free and pure man," this pattern is generally characterized by sporadic references to the novelist as an independent critical temperament, a rebel whose source of indignation and cynicism are the inadequacy and hypocrisy of contemporary culture; whose dynamic quest for honesty and truth leads him to a frenetic protest against all established convention - against the vulgar way that contemporary culture tries to mask its inadequacy through empty ideas and meaningless ideology. Baroja is the anguished individual whose pervasive anathema and sneering are aimed at the general emptiness of modern life. This pattern of references to an "incorruptible" Baroja finally jells in Ortega's concept of the novelist as something similar to sincerity personified, and it is this concept of sincerity, Ortega's essential intuition of Baroja, that is the "coordinating axis of his soul, his art, his life."

And so it is that Ortega succeeds in isolating "the generic object" of his second chapter: the "latent affinity" between Baroja's most intimate self and "a portion of the universe" is his affinity for sincerity, the generic object which is the motivating force behind all of Baroja's art, "the coordinating axis" of contemporary semiology.

Having understood Baroja through the identification of an essential pattern, Ortega, faithful to his own criterion for judging literature, had now earned the privilege to judge Baroja's art, and proceeds to do so in a chapter titled "On Baroja's Art," where, ironically enough, he relates Baroja's praiseworthy "essence" - for sincerity is no longer associated with babbling as it was in 1910 - to certain shortcomings in the novelist's art: to its inability to hold us in a convincing grip, among other things. For it is precisely the sincerity of our "free and pure man" which compels him to a certain impetuousness, a certain lack of patience, a certain haste to criticize which is in turn responsible for incomplete

35

characterization as well as for a lack of dramatic unity in Baroja's work. It is for this reason that Ortega concludes that Baroja's art would have profited a great deal had he tempered his sincerity with "pure contemplation," modified it with the artist's "primary imperative," - no longer a moral imperative -, which is to "look carefully at the world around him," with "_amor intellectualis._"

Now as well-intentioned students of Ortega, as good "spectators," it might behoove us to extricate ourselves from his multiple circles and to turn our backs, establishing some distance between ourselves and the circles in order to "complete," to "fill in" the meaning of Ortega's meditation on Baroja through a synthetic statement relating the three principal themes of his essay. The statement might read as follows: the critic whose correct purpose is to teach us _how_ to read what we are reading, himself properly inspired by _amor intellectualis_, will cull out and identify the essential aspect of the author being read, which in the example of Baroja is a wholesome, yet flagrant insubordination which leads to a frenetic haste not consonant with the patient reflection required for great art. In this sense, we can conclude that Baroja was not himself a very dedicated phenomenologist but rather a very impetuous romantic.[25]

Our next circle of attention has its inspirational source in the work of Fyodor Dostoyevsky, who, after Cervantes, was probably Ortega's predilect novelist, and one whose works allowed our philosopher to practice his "love" with superb results.

Scattered references to Dostoyevsky can be traced in Ortega's work beginning in 1913 and continuing through 1927, but the most important of these commentaries appear in 1915 and in 1924, in a very brief article on the new interest in baroque art, and in a brief chapter on Dostoyevsky and Proust which forms part of the more strictly phenomenological "Ideas on the Novel," the piece in which all of Ortega's meditations on the novel seem to crystallize in a unified display of analytic brilliance.

The 1915 piece titled "The Will of the Baroque,"[26] which includes some comments on the novel which anticipate the controversial pronouncements of 1924, is essentially an effort to explain a certain renascent attraction to baroque art, using as examples of this attraction in Ortega's contemporaries the work of Dostoyevsky, Stendhal, and El Greco, all of whom display distinct baroque tendencies, according to Ortega.

After informing his reader that the novel, which he refers to as a "positivist literary genre," thus repeating what he had said in _Meditations_, as well as anticipating once again what he would say in "Ideas," Ortega proceeds to explore, as an exception, the renewed and increasing popularity of Dostoyevsky, among others. This continuing popularity is related to a new interest in baroque art.

With respect to the Russian novelist, "the great Slav," Ortega's point of focus is what we can call the inner dynamics of Dostoyevsky's art, to the strict exclusion of all factors not related to this core problem of the structure of his art as such.

While Dostoyevsky writes in an age basically preoccupied with realism, it turns out that his art, according to Ortega, notwithstanding its ostensible affinity with the real world, its apparent concession to verisimilitude, owes its success precisely to its ability to displace the material primacy of things by substituting in their place an uncommon dynamism, an inner turbulence, which is the essence of "the exclusively poetic world which Dostoyevsky brings to the novel."

While the novelist's characters are inevitably caught up in apparently "real" movements, or "whirlwinds" such as debauchery, avarice, eroticism, perversion, etc., the connection between these "real souls" and exterior reality is minimal, and Ortega concludes his discussion of a baroque Dostoyevsky as follows:

> But the style of Dostoyevsky consists precisely in not fixing our attention on the material employed, but situating us, clearly, in the presence of pure dynamisms. It is not innocence as such, but rather the vital movement within it that makes up the poetic objectivity of The Idiot. For this reason, the most concise definition of a novel by Dostoyevsky would be to sketch, with an impetuous arm, an ellipse in the air (404).[27]

The sequel to this 1915 piece in which Ortega isolates and identifies the baroque aspect of Dostoyevsky's art appears nine years later, in the form of a condensed reflection on the essential structure of the fiction of Dostoyevsky and Proust, a brief section from "Ideas on the Novel," some four pages which should be read as a companion essay.[28]

The theme of the increasing popularity of Dostoyevsky's fiction in face of the virtual decline of the novel as a whole is also the subject of the first few paragraphs of the pages in question, as once again Ortega seeks to explain Dostoyevsky's magnetism through an uncompromising, exclusive assessment of the material between the covers of Dostoyevsky's books, through unrelenting focus on the object of his love and attention, through strict, although unstated, loyalty to the

37

phenomenological dictum "to the things themselves." In this case "the thing itself" is variously referred to by Ortega as "structure," "inner structure," "form," "the organism," which, he insists, is the object on which literary criticism should concentrate.

In these same initial paragraphs, consonant with what he had said in his 1915 inquiry into the secret of Dostoyevsky's continuing appeal during an age of disinterest in fiction, Ortega again stresses the virtual insignificance of subject matter in Dostoyevsky'a art, ascribing to it a very minimal role in the high, compelling, elusive structural drama which characterizes the fiction of the Russian novelist and which in turn explains his success. This structural drama is now not so much baroque, although baroque dynamics are implicit in everything Ortega says, as it is characterological. And characterology, as I hope to explain, seems to be the one missing ingredient, a bare outline in a recurring pattern which, as a potential unifying element, a coordinating axis, the reader must isolate and identify in order to "complete" the meaning of the otherwise vexing, albeit highly incisive fragments, the deceptively autonomous circles which form the individual chapters of Ortega's "Ideas on the Novel."

To return for the time being to the matter at hand, Ortega expresses his surprise at the fact that critics of the novel have been unable to see that form itself, "the structure of the novel as such," is its essence, and are consequently destined to suffer "a curious optical illusion" (similar to the one suffered by Ortega during his first critical phase?), ascribing to Dostoyevsky himself the demoniacal turbulence of his characters. An alert mind, however, one in quest of clarity, does not take this fantasy seriously, for the unknown fact is, according to Ortega, that Dostoyevsky was something quite contrary to what his readers and critics thought he was:

> It may be quite true that Dostoyevsky
> the man was an unfortunate, possessed soul,
> or, if one prefers, a prophet; but the
> novelist Dostoyevsky was a man of letters, a
> serious craftsman of an admirable craft,
> nothing more. I have often tried to convince
> Baroja, without entirely succeeding, that
> Dostoyevsky was, above anything else, a
> prodigious technician of the novel, one of
> the greatest innovators of fictional form
> (400).

With this assessment of an intellectual Dostoyevsky as master craftsman, as master technical innovator, Ortega seems to dispel what we might call the romantic legend of a monomaniacal deviate whose exclusive obsession was an irresistible roulette wheel, and sets the stage for an eidetic intuition of the basic structure of the formidable art of Dostoyevsky's fiction, of the structure of his art as art.

The readjustment of the natural or common viewpoint, or the removal of mental barriers, is the prerequisite which frees Ortega for the application of the eidetic methodology necessary for the achievement of pure transparency, the unraveling before his eyes of the latent pattern of characterization which is the crux of Dostoyevsky's fiction.

The intuition itself, achieved after the required reflective labor, a formidable chore in itself, is the revelation of a stratagem - a kind of cruel hoax - used by Dostoyevsky for the express purpose of locking his reader into the novel, at a safe distance from the natural world, confining him within what he is forced to accept as the "real" world of fiction.

When Dostoyevsky introduces a character, according to Ortega, he almost always provides a biographical sketch which the reader accepts as a definition, when in fact this is part of the novelist's entrapment of his reader in a dynamic, confusing struggle to formulate his own definition of what turns out to be a highly equivocal character.

When the ensuing behavior of this character begins, as it inevitably does, to clash with the initial "definition," the entrapment of the reader also begins, for, apprehensive of making a mistake with respect to his own image of the ambiguous character, the reader is forced into a determined, relentless pursuit of any action or conversation which might help him clarify an otherwise equivocal, elusive personage.

And so it is that we might say that the reader, having "bracketed out" the real world around him through exclusive attention to enigmatic fictional creatures, nevertheless approximates a real life situation in becoming the author of his own characters, although Ortega does not state it this way. The following excerpt from his pages on Dostoyevsky serves as a key synthetic statement:

> We consequently arrive at an unexpected conclusion: Dostoyevsky's "realism" - let us call it that in order to avoid complicating the matter - does not reside in the things and facts referred to by him, but rather in the manner in which the reader is forced to treat these things. It is not the matter of

life which constitutes his "realism," but rather the form of life (401).

So much for Ortega's application of phenomenology to Dostoyevsky and his unquestionable success, in this case, in helping us to see what stands before us, by exposing to our full view the novelist's essential form, through an essential intuition regarding characterization, although this matter is more complicated than my brief exposition may indicate.

Of equal or greater interest may be the fact that over and beyond his extraordinary technical expertise in character portrayal, Dostoyevsky seems to be an outstanding paradigm of an artist whose work satisfies any and all the criteria for a great novel as these are set forth in the interdependent, miniature circles which are the individual chapters of the inappropriately titled "Ideas on the Novel." For, although half-stated, perfunctorily alluded to during the course of his elliptical insight into the structure of Dostoyevsky's art, there is latent, on the periphery of this insight, a conclusion, to be supplied by Ortega's reader, that Dostoyevsky's work represents the eiptome of the "autoptic," "presentative," "sluggish," "provincial," "dense," "hermetic" qualities which are the hallmark of all great fiction and which, in turn, it should be stressed, are essentially related to skill in characterization, the sine qua non of the novel.

A single statement clarifying the obfuscated relationship between Dostoyevsky's characterization and the fundamental concepts expounded in "Ideas on the Novel" can be formulated as follows: Dostoyevsky's unique way with fictional beings is the key requisite which allows him to create an "autoptic," "slow" novel which, despite, or because of, its density - mainly the result of the endless conversation with which the writer stuffs his pages - rivets the attention of its reader to that ideal point where he shuts off the world around him and lives "hermetically sealed" within the confines of the novel itself, in perpetual, anxious pursuit of the blurred, yet "real," convincing characters of fiction.29

Since this same relationship between characterization and other aspects of the novel is present on a broader scale throughout "Ideas on the Novel," it becomes possible for Ortega's reader to "see" this essay in a unified way, by looking at the individual chapters of this vexing circle as a homologous perspective whose potential integrator is the depiction of humans in a fictional world and the impact of this depiction on the human reader in his natural world.

The crux of the problem is that all the while that our
attention is totally absorbed by such seductive concepts as
"autopsy," "hermetism," etc., we tend to lose sight of the
unifying motif, the latent unifying pattern persistently lurking
in the background, inauspiciously, throughout "Ideas." Yet these
core concepts, in one way or another, all relate inevitably to
characterization. An example or two from Ortega's individual
reflections should suffice to illustrate this point.

In the chapter titled "Autopsy," which terminology we must
understand in the etymological sense of self-revealing, the
concept of the autoptic novelistic method itself eclipses the
fact that Ortega is really talking about what we can now call
"autoptic characterization," or even "autoptic presentation," as
opposed to traditional description, definition, narration. In
the brief, three-paragraph "Autopsy," Ortega uses four different
novelists to illustrate his point regarding the essence of a
"presentative novel." In each of these four cases, Balzac,
Stendhal, Emilia Pardo-Bazán, and Cervantes, Ortega is really
discussing the "presentation," as opposed to representation, of
human characters and events as these are depicted in the
fictional environment.

The laurels go to Stendhal and Cervantes, while the less
fortunate Balzac and his Human Comedy turn out to be a mere sham,
and Pardo Bazán is perfunctorily dismissed.

With respect to Balzac, Ortega prefaces his evaluation with
reference to an "ocular apparatus" accustomed to authenticity,
one which easily detects the falseness in Balzac, and concludes,
through an analogy to painting, that Balzac's work is mere
allusion to things as opposed to the revelation of "authentic
presence."30

Pardo Bazán is rather summarily dismissed with the curt
observation that she tells us over and over again that a
particular character is witty, without ever allowing us to see it
by ourselves, without ever autoptically unfolding this wit before
our eyes, I shall add. The conclusion to Ortega's brief
rejection of Pardo Bazán, which contains unavoidable reference to
character depiction, no matter how oblique or obscured by other
considerations, reads as follows:

> The imperative of the novel is autopsy.
> It should contain no reference to what a
> character is: we need to see this with our
> own eyes (391).

Stendhal, on the other hand, measures up to the presentative
or autoptic craft which Ortega considers the novel's imperative

because he has a different way with fictional characters. Once again, the example used to illustrate Ortega's main point involves the depiction of humans in fiction: Julian Sorel and Madame Renal are in love, yet the reader is never told this, but rather put in a position where he discovers it himself, since Stendhal presents this relationship in "its immediate and patent reality."

And as we might well expect now, Cervantes is a paramount phenomenon in this respect, a master of the autoptic method, "one who saturates us with the pure presence of his characters."

In the chapter from "Ideas" titled "Hermetism," this inevitable reference to genuine character portrayal is even more difficult to discern, being as it is almost totally obscured by Ortega's compelling analysis of the novel as an alternate world in which, if the novel is to succeed, the author, "a divine somnambulist," and the reader alike, afflicted by a fertile somnambulance, exist exclusively within the strict confines of the novel itself, oblivious to the external natural world.[31] Nevertheless, the obscure yet inevitable reference does appear, once again clothed in the form of an illustration, as it becomes clear that the somnabulism referred to is really the craft of original human portrayal, or the portrayal of "men and women, speech and passions," etc.

As I have already indicated, such is the case throughout the analytic masterpiece "Ideas on the Novel," in which characterization is manifest in a kind of substratum form, yet nonetheless detectable, a fact which might now afford us the liberty to change Ortega's title to "The Novel as Anaturalistic Characterization," thus escaping the initial misdirection inherent in "Ideas on the Novel," and even moreso in the poor standard English version "Notes on the Novel." It is a fact that these circles are much more than "notes."

All directions really point to characterization, and, in this sense, especially if we decide to focus our "ocular mechanism" properly, the concluding words of "Ideas on the Novel," in the context of the novel, are of no small importance:

> The interest itself in the external mechanism of plot is today necessarily reduced to a minimum. So much the better for focusing the novel on the higher interest which may emanate from the internal mechanism of characters. Not in the invention of "actions," but in the invention of interesting souls do I see the brightest future of the novelistic genre (418).

The work of Marcel Proust is yet another "object of reflection" in "Ideas on the Novel," as it is in the 1923 piece "Time, Distance and Form in the Art of Proust."[32] I shall first treat Ortega's 1923 practical phenomenological exercise and conclude my discussion of Proust in Ortega by relating this essay to Ortega's observations as these appear two years later, in both "Dehumanization" and "Ideas."

Once again, the object of Ortega's longer article on Proust is to make his reader "see" the work of a novelist as it stands before his eyes, through its inner structure. And once again, as was most notably the case with Ortega's 1916 essay on Baroja, the piece on Proust is prefaced by an implicit defense of consciousness of the object itself as method, this time not with emphasis on critical method, but rather with theoretical emphasis on the role of consciousness as novelistic method. We can conclude from what Ortega says about Proust in his preface to "Time, Distance and Form," although it is never made explicit, that Proust himself was an eminent phenomenologist.

Proust, whose technique is analogous to the technique of impressionist painting, is a discoverer or "inventor" of a new esthetics in fiction owing to the fact that he was a maximal example of what Ortega refers to as "visual enthusiasm," one of a class of Platonic "philotheamones," or philosophers who are "lovers of looking."

As opposed to writers of little consequence who inherit a "determined posture," Proust belongs to a class of writers whose accomplishments in art are analogous to the accomplishments of "scientific discoverers" who unearth new objects by looking beyond the accepted perception of things, seeing them in a new way by adjusting to a "simple optic law" which results in an "unusual refraction."

I shall first make a synoptic statement on the originality of the great French pioneer as this is presented in the circle "Time, Distance and Form," and then proceed to discuss at some greater length the way in which Ortega relates Proust's radical decision with respect to the treatment of time to the consequent treatment of space and their ensuing manifestation in the inevitable prolix, diffuse, static quality which is the essence of Proust's form: Proust's radical inversion of the acquired way of treating time and space is the precondition for the microscopic diffusion which is responsible for the desirable, although fatiguing, adramatic tempo lento which is his novel.

Those novelists predating Proust who treated memory of the past in an effort to reconstruct it, did so in a fraudulent way,

43

for, given the disadvantage of the inherent incompleteness of their memory, they resorted to the present to complete their reconstruction. The author of the revolutionary A la recherche du temps perdu, on the other hand, determined to avoid all constructivism, was not so much interested in reconstructing the past as he was in reconstructing his memory of it as memory. Thus, Proust becomes, in the words of Ortega, an "investigator of lost time as such," enriching the tradition of the memoir with "the dignity of pure literary method."

Even more startling for its simplicity, according to Ortega, is Proust's inversion of distance in fiction. Fed up, perhaps, with the large-scale representation of things such as a hand, as a hypothetical example, the "delightfully myopic genius" narrows the spatial gap between viewer and hand to the point where the hand blots out the surrounding horizon,[33] thus affording him the advantage of perceiving the hand as such, in all its suggestive, microscopic array of pores, creases, etc., crowned by a fuzz which is referred to as a "Liliputian jungle," an obvious reference to the novelistic device used by Jonathan Swift.

The consequences of this radical change in perspective in fiction are inevitable for, having inverted time and space, Proust, determined to stay within the limits of his inversion, has no other recourse, with respect to time, than to stuff his pages with the minute details necessary for the fullest restoration of his memory as such, while with respect to space a similar situation is dictated: the observer's exclusive proximity to the things themselves forces him to confront them from a microscopic perspective, from which there is no other alternative but to elaborate on their essence through repeated reference to their minutest components.

Thus it is that Proust's art, which at one point Ortega refers to as "psychological pointillism," stressing its affinity with the diffuse atmospheric quality of impressionism, is destined to its characteristic form, that "sluggishness" which excludes reference to external reality and human drama as such, that principal barometer for measuring good fiction which appears again two years later in "Ideas on the Novel." Nothing really ever happens in Proust's novels, but so much the better, even though he is fatiguing, yet never boring.

The commentary on Proust found both in "The Dehumanization of Art" and "Ideas on the Novel," companion essays whose relationship I shall try to formulate as the conclusion of this chapter, can be viewed as an addendum and refinement of what Ortega had said in the piece on the French novelist discussed above.

In the chapter from "Dehumanization" titled "Supra and Infrarealism," the primary stress on microscopic detail is explicitly referred to as a "dehumanizing" instrument, in the sense that it inverts the normal order of things by delving beneath the surface of the natural perspective. Novelists who approach the microstructure of life "with lens in hand" include Ramón Goméz de la Serna, James Joyce, and Proust. The latter's kinship with the "new sensibility" in art might be explained, Ortega concludes, by the change in perspective which illustrates his utter disdain for the depiction of "monumental forms of the soul" and his "inhuman attention" to the finer structure of sentiment, human relations, characters.

In "Ideas on the Novel" Proust's extreme "sluggishness" becomes the focus of Ortega's meditation on two different occasions, once in his chapter on Dostoyevsky and Proust, and then again in the ensuing chapter titled "Action and Contemplation." As the superlative example of tempo lento in the novel, Proust's art, or what I shall now refer to as his "inhuman art," is exemplary to a fault: radically devoid of any human drama, it has the effect of suspending its reader in a purely contemplative state, yearning for that requisite minimal slice of human action which, according to Ortega, would have made of Proust's work the perfect novel. We might note in passing that Proust represents an ideal fictional example of Ortega's concept of dehumanization in painting, and that this fact provides an initial clue to the difficult problem of relating "Dehumanization" to "Ideas."

One more curious discussion of Proust in Ortega, dated 1939, communicates the impression, at first glance, that it is atypical of Ortega's maturer period, in that the discussion skirts the issue of Proust's art as such, the inner poetics of his fiction, the general practical rule of thumb which characterizes Ortega's criticism between 1913 and 1927. Yet the fact of the matter is that this apparent departure from the critical norm coincides with a general waning interest in practical immanent criticism which becomes apparent following Ortega's encounter with Heidegger in 1928, after which date Ortega's interest in art in general is displaced by a more exclusive interest in strict philosophy, in phenomenological pursuit of the essence of humans as opposed to the essence of their art, in pursuit of life itself as radical reality. I shall return to this change in direction and its consequences with respect to Ortega's criticism at a more appropriate juncture in the concluding chapter of this study. Suffice it to add for the time being that Ortega's final reference to Proust, when viewed chronologically, is not as atypical as it may first seem. The reference itself appears in a posthumously published philosophy of sociology titled Man and People, during a disquisition into interindividual relations and

the perspective from one's own world versus that of "the other."
In this context Proust is extolled as a genius whose radical
insight into life led him to the precise metaphorical equation,
expressed in the very titles of his tracts on Swann and
Guermantes, of the "technical terminology needed for the
formulation of a scientific theory of life."[34] Once again,
Ortega returns to the use of literary material for extraliterary
purposes, an apparent throwback to his early development, with
the difference that his third period is characterized not by an
interest in the communal and political welfare of humans, but
rather by a stricter ontological inquiry into the meaning of the
human creature itself.

While Ortega does not apply his phenomenological lens to
Stendhal with the same enthusiasm that he does in the cases of
the other novelists discussed above, Stendhal's name appears with
considerable frequency throughout his works, to a point where we
can trace chronologically the trajectory of Ortega's critical
thinking through these references in much the same way as we have
traced it in the cases of Azorín and Baroja.

Beginning in 1904, in the most mature of Ortega's pre-
phenomenological pieces, the one dealing with the magnificent art
of Valle Inclán, Ortega makes perfunctory reference to Stendhal
as a disdainful anachronist, while in his 1910 article on Baroja,
during the course of interpreting Baroja's aggressive
impertinence as a sign of personal timidity, he refers to
Stendhal as the Spaniard's "master," attributing the energetic
explosiveness of the French novelist to similar motives, to the
masking of his own insecurity. In this same article, Ortega
censures Stendhal for his unbridled anarchy.[35]

It seems that Ortega did not really begin to "see" Stendhal
until about 1917, during the second stage of his development,
when he was most prone to treating literature for what it is, and
little more, if anything. During that year, in his celebrated
piece on Azorín, Ortega points to Stendhal, among others, as an
example of a heroic, creative vitality whose dynamic
tumultuousness serves to displace reality.[36] This displacement
of reality in art is highly desirable, I shall add here.

This provides us with a convenient transition to the more
substantial comments on Stendhal made in "Ideas" in 1924, where
all novelistic criteria are related to the displacement of the
natural world around us. Stendhal is not only an excellent
example of "presentative" fiction, as I have already mentioned in
my discussion of the autoptic method, but additionally satisfies
the other basic requirements for a great novel: his work stands
as one of the foremost examples of the "sluggishness" and very
minimal action necessary for the detailed portrayal of an

alternate "real" world in fiction, with the result that the attention of Stendhal's reader is exclusively fastened to his pages, and nowhere else.[37]

Aside from defining Stendhal as the "archnarrator" of all time, Ortega says practically nothing about his art as such in the 1926 piece titled "Love in Stendhal," which is really an inquiry into one of Ortega's predilect topics, the concept of love. Part of the express purpose of this article is to demonstrate that Stendhal, like his colleague Baroja, notwithstanding his talent as a novelist, was not quite the philosopher which he and his public fancied him to be, for a "head full of theories" does not necessarily qualify as true philosophy. In particular, Stendhal's theory of love as "crystallization" is really a falsification of love.[38]

Anatole France is yet another French novelist whose name appears in Ortega's work intermittently over a period of some two decades. Reference to this writer culminates in the form of the complete piece titled "Reading Anatole France's Petit Pierre," published in 1919.[39] Although Ortega exposes his general admiration for and wide familiarity with the works of France, he is not nearly as generous with this novelist as he is with Proust and Stendhal.

"Reading Petit Pierre" leaves one with the feeling that it is an atypically impressionistic piece, a parenthetical surrender perhaps to the latent subjective tendency inherent in the phenomenological method. And it is Ortega himself who warns us not to expect strict literary criticism in his rather fanciful preamble to his essay, where he speaks, among other things, of the "spontaneous resonances" inspired by the reading of France's novel, on which he decides to expound with book closed.

The result is a personal overview of the writer which is generally a departure from the critical norms so fervently defended and applied by Ortega during his second stage of development, a brief transgression from the ideal of the inner structure itself as the object of consciousness.

The main thrust of Ortega's piece on France is that during a prolific span of some four decades, from Sylvestre Bonnard to Le Petit Pierre, the novelist in question had demonstrated little, if any, evolution. In pointing to what we can call the static quality of France's art, Ortega stresses his objection to what he considers the dull sameness of ideas, emotions, and technique which characterize the "precious literary ceramics" of an author who addressed his work to mediocre readers, to "philistines of culture."

47

Curiously enough, and rather unexpectedly, Ortega tries to buttress his case against France by contraposing the rational, geometric, static perfection of the novelist's art and the essential nature of the life drama itself, the dynamics of vitality and decay, with the resulting conclusion that France's art leaves much to be desired since it is not a legitimate reflection of what really transpires in human life, defined at one point as a "frenetic sculptor" who chisels his way toward an inexorable conclusion. During the course of his argument, Ortega clearly announces his preference for "an art more saturated with life."

Needless to say, especially when we consider the date of the article in question, this extraliterary judgment of a prose writer is an exception to the rule, for with the publication of Meditations in 1913 and continuing for some fourteen years until 1927, Ortega had generally remained fiercely loyal to the dictum "the thing itself," as well as to its concomitant severance from the natural life world. Thus, what is most impressive about his essay on France is the fact that Ortega's personal indulgence led him not only to stray from the standard of the novelist's art as such, but in addition to judge this art from within the framework of the natural standpoint, both anathema for the orthodox phenomenologist.

Yet, instead of viewing this brief interlude as a throwback to Ortega's early stage, it is perhaps more reasonable to conjecture that "Reading Petit Pierre" is an anticipation of that final stage of development where the literary text becomes a pretext for a more compelling ontological disquisition.[40]

Chronologically, Ortega's final piece on a single novelist appears in the form of a review in 1927 on The Leprous Bishop, a novel by the elegant mannerist Gabriel Miró.[41] The review is of interest both for its assessment of Miró's art, as well as for what it has to say about the novel in general.

In his assessment of Miró, whom he finds difficult to read, Ortega sounds somewhat like he sounds in his judgment of Anatole France. While acknowledging that Miró is indeed a great writer, Ortega is nevertheless reluctant to agree that he is even a good novelist, for the novel, that most difficult of all art forms, according to Ortega, is much more than simple esthetic perfection, no matter how splendid its language. With respect to this judgment on the secondary role of lyricism in the novel, it can be said that between his 1904 essay on Valle Inclán and the 1927 piece on Miró which marks the end of his speculating on such matters, Ortega had demonstrated no change in his attitude, prone as he was from beginning to end to censuring estheticism in prose fiction for the sake of estheticism. Yet there is a difference

48

in the standard used to censure in his early period and the one used in his second period, for whereas the young Ortega deprecated style for its own sake as a way of underscoring the resulting absence of human values in such art, the more mature Ortega criticizes prose estheticism for reasons pertaining to the novelistic form itself, as the case of Miró illustrates.

Most of Ortega's objection to his fiction proceeds from the idea of characterization and its relationship to verisimilitude. As an example, Ortega cites the incongruent, flowery literary metaphor which typifies the speech of an otherwise humble village priest, a principal figure in The Leprous Bishop. The problem is not so much one of a lack of verisimilitude per se, which is really of no importance, according to Ortega, but rather a problem of "the esthetic verisimilitude" which is the "internal congruence of the microcosm created by the author," much more important, as we might expect by now, than the mere coincidence of a book with the natural world around us.

The fact of the matter is, Ortega affirms, that Miró's internal incongruency is most apparent in the example of the good padre since his speech, within the novel itself, clashes with the other fictional characteristics ascribed to him, thus making of him a contrived being as opposed to a genuine one.

And such defective characterization is a general problem in Miró, for the Spanish novelist creates types instead of individuals, being as he is the victim of a temptation common among novelists. His characters ring false because of an underlying conventionalism which stems from his willingness to sketch an average or aggregate drawn from common, vulgar experience and to sacrifice the direct vision of reality to this mediocre average.

Yet this is not to deny, Ortega continues, that all individuals belong to one type or another, and in this sense it is incumbent upon the novelist to make at least a partial concession to the real world by creating some sort of recognizable type. However, this type must be the exception to the rule, an extraordinary type who stands much above the vulgar norm. Such a character, drawn from the profoundest layers of reality, must differ radically from the generic type already known to the reader. Since Miró does not meet this standard, we can conclude, once again, that he is a great writer who does not know how to write novels.

As I have indicated, Ortega's article on Miró marks the end of rather keen interest in the work of individual prose writers, an interest which was translated into its optimal expression between the years 1913-1927, when Ortega was at his best at attending, almost exclusively, to the personal experiencing of the object of his attention, which, with respect to literary criticism, was almost always the novel as novel. In addition, the year 1927 marks the end of that special morphological approach to works of art in general, an approach that can be alternately described as a primary focus on the inner logic of the work of art itself.

Beyond its unquestionable importance as a general assessment of the radical innovations in painting during the early decades of this century, "The Dehumanization of Art" can also be viewed as a general manifesto which synthesizes the theoretical position which structures all the practical literary criticism published by Ortega between 1913 and 1927.

A normal, as opposed to a closer reading of the introductory paragraph of "Dehumanization" would, with little doubt, lead the reader to the conclusion that the references to Guyau contained in the paragraph in question are merely cursory references used by Ortega as a point of departure for the elaboration of a more compelling polemic which has little or no connection with Guyau's work itself.

Yet, in point of fact, despite its ostensible function, the real meaning of this introduction is that it represents a subtle, veiled, ironic rejection of the sociological norms which guided Guyau's pronouncements on the art of his contemporaries, those very same norms which guided Ortega's abrasive judgement of his own contemporaries as either dangerous Mediterranean sensualists or effete, disengaged nightingales whose lack of interest in the human community disqualified them as legitimate artists. In this sense, the introduction to "Dehumanization" should be approached as a kind of muted announcement on the part of Ortega that he would parade before the public eye what had by then become an irrevocable decision in favor of a clear, radical break from the preceptive communal ideals which were the structuring force behind his inquiries into art during his early period, to the extent that the strict formalism of "Dehumanization" would represent the maximally refined, culminant expression of the willful displacement of all esthetic values by what is essentially inhuman in art, by disengaging, desocializing, severing it from all human contingency, by "dehumanizing" it.

When Ortega states that Guyau's <u>Art from a Sociological Point of View</u> "is yet to be written," he means that he intends to write such a book himself, but in precisely the reverse sense in which Guyau had intended his work: he means that he, Ortega, will proceed to demonstrate that what is true about art in its sociological context is precisely the inverse of what Guyau had said of art and sociology; that art and social values, however remote, simply cannot cohabit, and that in fact a true sociology as reflected in the history of taste reveals that it is precisely the type of art which is translatable into social or human terms, especially the art of the nineteenth century, and this includes romanticism as well as realism, which is a monstrous counterfeit whose popularity alone stands as ample proof of its illegitimacy.

We might say, then, that Ortega's "Dehumanization" is to his esthetics exactly what Husserl's "Philosophy as Rigorous Science" (1911) was to his epistemology, for both pieces represent a sweeping, synthetic, definitive decision on the absolute necessity of denaturalizing perception and cognition to that ideal point where the liberated subject is forced to approach his naked object "from the bottom up," to constitute the object itself through an essentialist epistemology which, in the case of Husserl, involved divesting himself of more than two thousand years of philosophy, while in the case of Ortega, divesting himself of the same number of years of esthetic speculation which was ultimately structured through contingency with the natural world, which inevitably meant the naturalistic adulteration of pure consciousness.

It is for this reason that the primary coefficient of naturalism, the naive realism which structures the taste of the myopic masses and without fail drives them to an art which is easily appreciated, becomes the focal point of Ortega's relentless, quite often gratuitous, sociological assault on the mediocre rabble whose radical lack of esthetic orientation compels it to reject the art of Cézanne and the post-impressionists; the amorphous mob whose strict allegiance to naturalism makes it impossible for it to assimilate "artistic art."

In this, as in many other respects, such as its aggressive tone, terminology, posturing, spirit, and theoretical disquisitions, "Dehumanization" is strikingly comparable to Clive Bell's Art, that other aggressive formalist milestone on Cézanne and the post-impressionists, first published in 1914, a decade prior to the publication of its companion, "Dehumanization."

When Ortega contraposes "artistic" or "dehumanized" art with the "lived" or "human reality" which thoroughly saturates the second-rate representation most characteristic of the nineteenth century, concluding that a preoccupation with the human content of art is in reality incompatible with esthetic enjoyment, clearly opting for an art which has rid itself of "the human pathos," or "the story of John and Mary" so popular among the unrefined rabble, he sounds like an echo of the English aristocrat whose elitist hypothesis, "significant form," is also contraposed to art bearing any resemblance to the nineteenth

51

century: Ortega's "artistic art" and Bell's "significant form" are one in the same in that they leave little or no room for the human interests and concerns of daily life, for the art which appeals to what Bell calls "the gross herd," "the mass of mankind," "the mediocre mass," etc.

Of the many passages at our disposal from Bell which clearly resemble Orteguian pronouncements, and which might well be ascribed to Ortega if one were unaware of their true source, the following may be considered typical:

> Be they artists or lovers of art, mystics or mathematicians, those who achieve ecstasy are those who have freed themselves from the arrogance of humanity. He who would feel the significance of art must make himself humble before it. Those who find the chief importance of art or of philosophy in its relation to conduct or its practical utility - those who cannot value things as ends in themselves or, at any rate, as direct means to emotion - will never get from anything the best that it can give. Whatever the world of aesthetic contemplation may be, it is not the world of human business and passion; in it the chatter and tumult of material existence is unheard, or heard only as the echo of some more ultimate harmony.[42]

As I have indicated, "Dehumanization" can be viewed as the culminant, most explicit theoretical pronouncement which illuminates virtually all the practical criticism published by Ortega between 1913 and 1927, for in one way or another, whether it was to indulge in Cervantes with an innocent retina, to "see" Azorín's universal microcosm, to unravel for his reader the essential Baroja, to convince him beyond doubt of the supreme craftsmanship of the compelling Dostoyevsky, to approach the microstructural world of Proust with an unadulterated lens, to discover the autoptic or "presentative" world of Stendhal, to voice his vehement opposition to traditional realism, Ortega unfailingly resorted in his critical methodology to the displacement or reversal of the natural order of material things, thus paralleling in his criticism the efforts of his contemporary partisans of the "new science" toward the same goal, toward the denaturalizing, including the dehumanizing, of all phenomena.[43]

Given the fact that the kinship between "Dehumanization" and "Ideas on the Novel" is much more implicit than it is apparent, our remaining task in this chapter is to formulate a statement clarifying the relationship between these two brilliant pieces.

When Ortega states in the key chapter from "Ideas" titled "Hermetism" that a novel "can be nothing beyond a novel," he comes closest to the explicit formulation of a parallel to what he had already said about painting and, for that matter, art in general, for a novel as "nothing beyond the novel" is the esthetic equivalent of what we can call painting as "nothing beyond painting," the basic precept which informs and structures the formalism behind "Dehumanization."

Among other things, the novel as nothing beyond a novel means that a novel is essentially its form, just as a painting is its form, to the virtual exclusion of all other considerations. And just as art is a thing "of no consequence," lacking in seriousness and transcendent importance, being as it is a contemplative sport or game, so might we say that the novel is a contemplative sport or game whose transcendental appearances are but a mere appendage to the self-sufficient world characteristic of what we call a great novel.[44] Beyond its conceding that minimal human action necessary to avoid the "paralytic novel," there is in the genuine novel no other concession to the real or natural world which is the actual world of the reader. This is so to the extent that, according to Ortega, novels worthy of their name generally succeed in imprisoning their readers within the confines of the novel, sealing them "hermetically" from the outside so as to convert them into "somnambulists." And the primary requisite for such a state of affairs in social disengagement, or estrangement, primarily in the sense that these terms and their opposites are used by the "committed" (engaged) philosophers of the novel such as Sartre:

> In this sense I would dare say that a
> novelist is one who has the gift of
> forgetting, and consequently making us
> forget, the reality he leaves out of his
> novel...this is why every novel laced with
> transcendental aspirations, be these
> political, ideological, symbolic, or
> satirical is stillborn. For these activities
> are of such a nature that they cannot be
> treated fictitiously, having meaning only in
> reference to the actual background of each
> individual (III, 411).

All this amounts to yet another echo of "dehumanization," although Ortega does not use this term in "Ideas." Yet as applied to the novel, dehumanization means, as it does with respect to painting, the almost total, radical exclusion from the novel of any human or natural element, and brings us close to the

53

antinaturalist position of "literariness" as this was espoused by the early formalists.[45]

Once again, the polemics in "Dehumanization" and "Ideas" are essentially one in the same in that they represent a rejection of naturalism and realism in favor of the genuine experiences of another world, one rather remotely related to the natural reality present to our eyes, the historical environing world of the Greeks and its strict representation, that common enemy of the phenomenologists.

CHAPTER III

POETRY AND THEATER

As the reader might expect by now, the esthetic
transcendentalism inherent in the early practical criticism
addressed to the prose works of figures such as Azorín, Baroja,
and Valle Inclán is equally manifest in the critical work which
the young Ortega addressed to poetry and theater, and was
reinforced, in the case of poetry, by theoretical speculation, as
well as implications, regarding the nature of metaphor.

One of the most significant of Ortega's early inquiries into
the nature of poetry, briefly treated in the first chapter of
this study, is the second chapter of "Maxims" titled "New Poetry,
Old Poetry" (1906), since this chapter stands in direct
contradiction to the strict formalism which became the hallmark
of the practical criticism published between 1913 and 1927. It
represents a far cry from the concept of art as an end in itself,
as a game or sport whose substance is its very structure, the
idea, in this case, of poetry as poetry, for in 1906 poetry was
everything that it was not during Ortega's second period.

The rather abrasive piece in question was inspired by the
publication of an anthology of modernist poets titled The Court
of Poets, and is a general assessment of the work of some fifty
writers. While conceding that art is a liberating activity, one
that helps free us from the daily humdrum of life, Ortega
nevertheless insists that poetry must be fully engaged with
life's paramount problems, and that it can never be justified as
pure esthetic. In fact, the poet who is not engaged, who does
not consider himself "responsible for the rectitude of his
esthetic," is not a poet at all, but rather "a philistine"
devoted, among other things, to the "splendor of the moon."

The primary focus of "New Poetry, Old Poetry" is the word,
and in discussing its proper function in poetry, Ortega clearly
distinguishes between the word as significant human value and the
word as value in itself, rejecting pure sonorousness and melody
as a norm. The following passage best sums up the fundamental
thrust of the chapter under discussion:

> Words are logarithms of things, images,
> ideas and feelings, and, consequently, can
> only be used as signs of values, never as
> values. The sonorous beauty of words is
> great at times...but this sonorous beauty is
> not poetic; it comes as a vestige of music,
> which makes us see in the components of a
> phrase an elemental melody. In brief, the

musicality of words is a very important source of esthetic pleasure in poetic creativity, but it is never the gravitational center of poetry.

The general attitude toward sensualism in verse becomes manifest as well in the young Ortega's criticism of individual poets, especially in a 1912 article on the great Spanish modernist Antonio Machado, which, as is the case with "New Poetry, Old Poetry," stands as one of the most important documents on art published during Ortega's first philosophic phase.[1]

Whereas the general evaluation of Spanish writers is usually a negative one, especially during Ortega's first period, Machado stands up quite well, and is, in fact, with some important reservations, an admirable poet according to the Spanish philosopher. And he is admirable precisely for reasons relating to his determination to communicate in meaningful human terms, to humanize the Castilian landscape and its history, to see the unifying force of man in all aspects of nature, much like the ancient, "eternally poetic" philosopher Anaxagoras. In this respect, Ortega is quite decidedly metaphysical in his criteria for judging Machado.

And yet the reservations are equally significant, for while the article on Machado does reveal a more moderate attitude toward sensualism than was previously the case, it nevertheless stops short of total approval, since the Spanish poet, who represents a solid beginning, a transitional phase toward a human poetry in a new key which is much more meaningful than the poetry of his contemporaries, still exhibits too much of the descriptive tendency of the decadent sensualists. While the transition represented by Machado is a huge step in the right direction, poetry, including the poetry of Machado, still needs to be cleansed of its self-indulgent estheticism:

But now we need more: the esthetic well-being of words, their unlimited capacity to express having been recovered, the substance of verse having been salvaged, it is necessary to resurrect its lyric soul. And the soul of poetry is the soul of the man who composes it. And this soul can never consist of the stratification of words, of metaphors, of rhythms. It must be a place where the universe breathes, a breathing organ for essential life, spiraculum vitae, as the German mystics would have it.[2]

Among the many brief references to both major and minor poets during this first philosophic phase, the references to the consummate Nicaraguan poet Rubén Darío and to Saint John of the Cross are the most significant.

With respect to Rubén, whose lavish, pioneering neo-romanticism is to the history of Spanish poetry what Valle Inclán's awesome prose is to the novel, Ortega's first reference, which appears in his first brilliant critical effort on Valle Inclán (1904), is a negative one. Noting the kinship between Valle Inclán's distaste for the transcendental, his fetishistic attraction to the word, his exaggerated mannerism, and the early work of the Nicaraguan dandy, Ortega properly associates both writers with the French symbolists, concluding that the work of all these writers, including that of minor writers influenced by these major figures, was more prejudicial to literature than it was useful.[3]

Yet of equal significance is the fact that during this same first phase of development, in 1908 and then again in 1911, Rubén becomes the object of praise, as one whose "place is assured in the heavens"[4] and as "the divine Indian," "a poetic forge," and "tamer of words," who led Spanish poetry out of the dismal prosaic realism into which it had fallen during the latter part of the nineteenth century.[5]

This apparent contradiction in Ortega's attitude toward Rubén is most probably explainable in terms of the two distinct directions that characterize the work of the poet. His early works, Blue (1888) and Profane Hymns (1896), steeped in French estheticism, are monuments of preciousness replete with delicate carnations, fine oriental silks, swans, and sad, pale, unique princesses. At the very least, it was unlikely that the young social-minded Ortega would become ecstatic over such exquisiteness.

A year after Ortega's initial perfunctory remarks on Rubén, however, in 1905, the Nicaraguan esthete had changed directions, publishing a collection whose title, Songs of Life and Hope, is indicative in itself: in this work the poet puts his musical gifts at the service of more universal, racial, political, and historical themes wherein fundamental human problems such as injustice become of paramount importance. The Neo-Kantian Ortega was most probably more attracted to this type of poetry than he was to the verse of the earlier Rubén, and it is against this background, I think, that the philosopher's changed attitude within the same developmental phase can be explained.

The rare genius of St. John of the Cross is yet one more target for assault during Ortega's formative years, and this assault is in turn yet one more confirmation of his rabid scorn for poetry which is not humanly engaged.

In 1909, in the same article in which he generally upbraids Unamuno for his insistence on things Spanish as opposed to things European, Ortega displays an inordinate reaction to the Basque's statement that given the choice between a Descartes and a St. John, he would opt for the latter. Ortega's answer to this type of scientific impropriety is a vehement, rather juvenile denouncement of the great Spanish mystic as a "pretty little friar of incandescent heart who wove laces of ecstatic rhetoric in his cell."[6] While this excessive reaction may in part be attributable to Unamuno's provocative statements, including his having labeled Ortega a "simpleton," it is nevertheless indicative, and coincides with Ortega's lifelong attitude toward mysticism in general.[7] In many ways, especially in their disengagement from the real world and in their inwardness, the mystics resembled esthetes.

In addition to the explicit references to individual poets and poetry in general published by Ortega during this period, there is also available to us a document on Renan (1909) in which Ortega provides further insight into the traditional norms used by him to judge poetry.[8] This insight comes in the form of his speculation on the nature of metaphor and its relationship to objective truth as opposed to subjective verisimilitude. While the essay on Renan is not as explicit as it might have been, during the course of Ortega's denouncement of "leprous subjectivity" (a statement which he calls "blasphemous" in a note appended in 1915), his defense of mathematical truth and his assessment of Renan's work as half-truth, what comes to the surface, mainly through association, is an implicit contempt for the metaphorical world which is not more strictly representational, more strictly logical.[9] Together with his attitude toward effeminate esthetes, Ortega's ideas on metaphor would undergo substantial change.

That these esthetes fair much better during Ortega's perspectivist period than they do during his Neo-Kantian phase is beyond question (the name of Proust comes immediately to mind), and the pieces on individual poets as well as on metaphor published between 1914 and 1927 stand as ample verification of the discovery of the intrinsic beauty of the word itself, the post-classical discovery of that maximal dehumanized splendor, the neutral, disengaged lyrical beauty of the very exquisite Mallarmé.

On the road to Mallarmé and the ornate Góngora, Ortega published separate essays on the Indian Nobel writer Rabindranath Tagore (1918) and the poetry of Ana de Noailles (1923), to whom he had some twenty years earlier dedicated a few pages. The essays on these two foreign poets offer ample evidence of Ortega's about face.

Ortega's piece on Tagore was inspired by the translation into Spanish by Zenobia Camprube, the wife of Juan Ramón Jiménez, of selected works by the Indian poet.[10] In this piece, in his opinions on Tagore and on poetry in general, as well as in his own rather sonorous style, Ortega leaves the reader with the curious impression that he himself had been converted into an immaculate romantic esthete, precisely of the type against whom he had unfailingly directed the vehement epithets of his early polemics.

In an unreal language embroidered by nymphs with blue eyes and blond clouds on their temples, Ortega, by the time of the publication in question some thirty-five years old, first describes poets as "furtive hunters of nymphs who cast fine crystaline threads on the fringes of reality," all in an effort, like spiders who weave fine nets, to capture only what is quintessential. And in the case of the poet, the quintessential object to be snared is the exquisite nymph, to the absolute exclusion, it should be emphasized, of all those other vulgar things which form the natural environment. The material world of the philistines must simply filter through the fine web without staining it in the least.

Such an exclusive hunter of nymphs is Tagore himself, according to Ortega, since, in the first place, aside from his other gifts, unlike the Spanish romantic Zorilla, whose fame can be attributed to his dramatic reliance on material objects such as castles, cathedrals, streets, etc., the mystical Tagore has absolutely no need of the particulars of time, place, or history to forge his splendid lyrics. In a word, Tagore's universality is anchored in a cloud, the sky, a spring, and other ephemera which torment him.

Ortega's romantic homage to Tagore's inwardness is substantially reinforced through several lengthy citations from the Spanish version of Tagore, as well as by his extensive commentary on these selected passages, whose presence speaks as clearly of Ortega's conversion as do his comments.

The first passage proffered by Ortega as irrefutable evidence of Tagore's universality is a story in itself. Written in an exclusively subjective first person, it describes Tagore's anguished quest for the self. The introspective pcet, like an antelope losing its sanity over its own scent, makes an agonizing effort to encounter his own shadow one night in May, to no avail. This unrequited quest, of course, causes him to become despondent, and he concludes by stating that he has what he does not want and wants what he does not have. All of which is highly stimulating to Ortega, who then adds that the reader's inability to localize the voice of Tagore is ample proof of the poet's universality. Be that as it may, we can safely conclude that by the time he had published his essay on Tagore, the Spanish philosopher was well on the transitional road to the ideas expressed in "Duhumanization," and more specifically, within this essay, on Mallarmé. Dehumanized self-indulgence had, by 1918, begun to appear in the form of nymphs, gazelles, and, in the remaining passages quoted from Tagore, perfumed garlands and inaccessible, utopian beauties who seem to have been plucked from the legends of a Bécquer.

Ortega's attraction to more remote poetic universes is also reflected in his enthusiasm for the neo-romantic stylism of the French poetess Ana de Noailles, whose voluptuousness and eroticism prompt him to compare her to Sappho. In "The Poetry of Ana de Noailles," an article inspired by the latest volume of verse by her,[11] Ortega additionally refers to Noailles as "the most poetic of countesses and the most countess of poetesses," while at the same time judging her as "the greatest spinstress of (contemporary) French lyricism."

This is largely so because this distinguished lady lives in a first person metaphorical world of "precious phantasmagoria" in which she compares herself to a wounded swallow; in which bellfries are sweet, argentine beehives; rain is a sun playing with metallic rays; stars are fragments of day in the limpid night, among other things.

Once again, as was the case with Tagore, Ortega buttresses his remarks on the poetess with numerous quotes from her work, this time quoting from the original French. These selected passages are as much a revelation as were the passages quoted from Tagore, for they too speak of unrequited love, of melancholy seasons, of perfumed gifts, gazelles, magnolia, camelia, and jazmine. The world of the Spanish modernists, absolute anathema to the pre-1914 Ortega, made eminent sense in an anguished French countess one decade after the critical turning point in his career.

A few months following his publication on Ana de Noailles, Ortega wrote a very brief recollection of what he experienced mentally during the occasion of his participation in a solemn homage to Mallarmé in the form of five minutes of silence, in the company of other distinguished intellectuals in the Botanical Gardens of Madrid.[12] In this fragment on Mallarmé, he clearly anticipated the Mallarmé of his "Dehumanization," the one who knew how to be a pure poet and nothing more, "the first man in the past century who wished to become a poet." "In what sense," Ortega asks in his recollection of the silent homage, "is the poetry of Mallarmé a type of eloquent silence?" He provides the answer as follows:

> It consists of suppressing the direct names of things, causing the inquiry into them to become a delightful enigma. Poetry is this and nothing more than this, and when it is something else it is neither poetry nor anything. The actual name denotes a reality, and poetry is, above all, a valiant flight, an arduous evasion of realities...the circus cyclist who races among bottles, avoiding contact with them. In totemist and magical epochs of culture, the individual had two names: one used socially, another - the real one - a secret, known only to his mother and father...Mallarmé is a linguist of this language composed solely of arcane and magical denomination.

Whereupon Ortega proceeds to relate these traits in Mallarmé to a similar evasiveness in Dante, quoting the latter fairly extensively in an effort to prove his point.

Yet there was more to come, for the final, definitive assessment of Mallarmé appears in the brief chapter of "Dehumanization" titled "The Dehumanization of Art Continues," which is in turn, significantly enough, followed by Ortega's chapter on taboo and metaphor.

That Mallarmé is a perfect paradigm of what poetry is or should be according to Ortega is made abundantly clear in the chapter from "Dehumanization" which now concerns us: Mallarmé is the first modern poet to discover poetry because he knew how to avoid the contagion of the natural world in the interest of becoming a pure, anonymous voice, creating, as opposed to involving himself with human circumstances and figures, non-vital resonances, and "figures so extraterrestrial that their contemplation is in itself a maximal pleasure." This poet was a true master of words, which had now become, in themselves, radically disjoined from human affiliation, "the true protagonists of lyrical enterprise." Ortega concludes his synthetic statement on Mallarmé with the summary statement that "poetry today is the higher algebra of metaphors,"[13] which is to say that by 1924, the metaphor which he had scorned during his youth had become the essence of poetry, that pure metaphor was indeed poetry, and that pure poetry was simply metaphor, of the type disengaged from concrete human reality, a cerebral exercise, or, once again, sport and game; the poet as cyclist, dodging bottles, and the world itself, hermetically sealed in a metaphor, as the genuine novelist is sealed in his world.

Ortega's final piece on a single poet, composed in 1927, the year which also marks the end of his interest in literature as such, was written as part of a homage organized by a coterie of proponents of "pure poetry" marking the tricentennial of the death of the baroque giant Luis de Góngora, whose florid elusiveness and metaphorical artifice are unmatched in the history of the Castilian language, and who, notwithstanding a concomitant obsession with vulgar degeneracy, is considered by many to be the greatest of Castilian poets.

The piece in question, "Góngora: 1627-1927" was composed under pressure of a deadline, and consequently comes down to us in the form of fragmentary notes which are sometimes fleeting impressions, as opposed to a coherent statement on Góngora.[14]

Nevertheless, despite this fragmentary quality, Ortega's hasty notes on the very cerebral Góngora, whose name he couples with that of Mallarmé and "the hieroglyphic mission of verse," can be viewed as further confirmation of his esthetic convictions, together with their phenomenological basis, as these appear in the more unified "Dehumanization." Once again, Ortega brings to the fore his virulent antinaturalism, insisting on the splendor of inhuman poetry which gleefully abandons itself to nymphs and swans, on poetry as euphemism, as unadulterated jocularity whose purpose is to dislocate the quotidian, the mundane.

This time, the dislocation of the natural world is put to the service of a more convincing argument with respect to poetry, for, while Ortega avoids phenomenological terminology per se, he nevertheless specifically relates his antinaturalism to an essentialist view of poetry in which the object of attention (and intention) is recreated in all its pristine, startling vitality; its revelation in its nascent state.

One of the most eminent European pioneers in this matter of metaphorical substitution for reality is Dante, for given his supremely oblique metaphorical skill, he was able to literally startle reality and recreate it in all its virginal splendor, forcing it to yield in the consciousness of the reader to all its nascent splendor.

And yet another pioneering phenomenologist of similar stock is the magical Góngora, for, endowed with but one eye, like Polyphemus himself, blind to the traditional way of communicating things as the centuries had forged them, he was able to elude their stagnancy, and to forge them anew through the metamorphic magic by which a bird becomes a tiny bell, a star becomes spring barley. Ortega concludes this portion of his notes on Góngora by announcing that "poetry has eternally consisted of substituting a cat for a hare."

I shall here take the liberty of translating in full one of the more significant passages on poetry by Ortega, although his notes on Góngora contain others which may be equally quotable:

> Poetry is not naturalness, but rather a will toward mannerism. Its history unfolds in its increasing capacity for mannerism. On occasions, its wings are fractured, and it relapses into prose, in order to once again begin its process of progressive distillation. On occasion, due to exclusive struggle in the wind, it vanishes in blue. Euphemism becomes unintelligible. Dante is a primary force, with his genteel style, and it was inevitable that European poetry should experience the extreme power of "cultured style." Centuries later, it was to return to nurture itself in these same spheres with Mallarmé. Whenever poetry elevates itself to such heights the classical fauna reappears, and it speaks of fawns, nymphs, swans; it plays with the gods.

The fact that Ortega ends his scattered notes on Góngora with an admonition to the younger poets to beware of Góngora's baroque excesses has little or no bearing on his overall view of this prince of poets.

The few pages by Morón-Arroyo on Ortega's changing attitude toward metaphor itself and the significance of this change with respect to his parallel modified attitude toward estheticism, have substantially facilitated my own work in this respect, to the point of enabling me to make a brief summary statement in closing these pages on Ortega as a critic of poetry.

The important publications on metaphor which follow the early-phase publication on Renan are "An Essay on Esthetics by Way of a Prologue" (1914), "Two Great Metaphors" (1924), and "Dehumanization" (1924). With respect to the concepts on metaphor in this latter essay, I have, it is hoped, already touched on them amply in my discussion of Mallarmé in Ortega.

"An Essay on Esthetics" may be viewed as a transitional work on metaphor, since, instead of being rejected as it was in the

63

case of "Renan," metaphor is now the esthetic object per se, a new object created through the transfiguration of another more common object via the medium of the "executive I," specifically, a cypress become flame, the new object which I experience vitally, "executively," since it has become a possibility through my willing it, through my sensing it.

In "Two Great Metaphors" the concept of the metaphor is advanced a step further: it is now fundamentally pure expression, in direct proportion to its ability to avoid the one-for-one substitution of concrete things, relying in their stead on psychology and emotion. Thus, metaphor becomes more ideally suited to cleanse itself of real things, and as pure creation, becomes a flight from reality. That same flight from reality, of course, that characterizes the poetry of Tagore, Noailles, and especially of Mallarmé and his predecessor, Góngora.[15]

While it is probably true, as I shall attempt to demonstrate, that the more important disquisitions by Ortega into the nature of the theater were written during the final phase of his development, after he had fallen under the spell of Heidegger, there is still adequate evidence to demonstrate that the writings on drama from his naturalist and anti-naturalist periods substantially parallel his writings on fiction and poetry from these same periods, although it seems true that he was less interested in drama than he was in the two latter genres.

The most important statement on a single playwright from Ortega's naturalist period, "The Poet of Mystery," dates from 1904, and is an inquiry into the early work of the Nobel anti-naturalist Maeterlinck, the outstanding exponent of symbolist theater. In this article, as we might reasonably expect, the social message once again comes to the fore.

After pointing to Maeterlinck's inwardness and suggestiveness as opposed to explicitness, the affinities of his work with music, in short, its general romantic dimensions, Ortega compares the playwright's work to the excesses of Spanish mysticism, whose melancholia, Ortega claims, was probably inherited by the Belgian writer as a result of the Spanish occupation of the Low Countries. He then concludes his article by censuring the type of estheticism which is steeped in vagueness and imprecision, with the advice that the reader beware of "meta-cosmic hallucinations." The symbolism of the early Maeterlinck, obviously, could not hold up under the early reasoning of a classical humanist.

Similar conclusions regarding the social values manifest in Ortega's early approach to the theater can be reached with respect to his treatment of Shakespeare, who, unlike Maeterlinck, was one of Ortega's predilect authors, mentioned frequently and favorably by the Spanish philosopher throughout his entire career.

The brief review titled "Shylock,"[16] published in 1910, is yet another instance of social criticism derived from a work of literature, written by Ortega as an angry protest a few days after witnessing a performance of the Merchant of Venice, which he interpreted as a radical misrepresentation of what Shakespeare really meant.

The Italian group responsible for this performance was guilty of a "collective crime," according to Ortega, for it was blind to the fact that great classical writers, like Shakespeare, steeped as they are in the real world, are "an invitation to historical humanity," as opposed to irresponsible excesses. The culprits had erred in emphasizing the negative qualities of Shylock, for in doing so, they helped reinforce the anti-semitic pestilence still rampant in an age that should understand the injustice and cruelty meted out to an anguished race of humans throughout history.

As was the case with Maeterlinck six years earlier, the author of "Shylock" had not yet learned to focus a pristine eye on theater as theater, as he would inevitably focus it in his discussion of Shakespeare and the theater in 1921, in an article inspired by the performance of "The Bat," a Soviet musical comedy in ballet form.[17]

In contrasting the purely plastic quality of the Russian piece, its dance, chorus, comical vignettes, etc., with traditional drama, Ortega defines Hamlet and most of Shakespeare's other work, with the exception of The Tempest, as well as traditional theater in general, as literature whose current presentation on the stage is quite superfluous. This is so because traditional drama is essentially a theater of words. Consequently, in order to experience its full impact, we need go no further than the written text, no further, especially in the case of that unique masterpiece of psychological portrayal, Hamlet, than its magnificent baroque eloquence - its written metaphorical elegance. As a matter of fact, hearing these written words emanating from common actors on stage can only serve to distort Shakespeare's Hamlet. The Tempest is an exception to this rule because it is a forerunner of pure spectacle, phantasmagorical artifice which one must witness if he is to enjoy it.

Similarly, works like "The Bat" are a harbinger of what the theater of the future should become: although Ortega does not use the words, he is really speculating on something that we can term "pure theater," the equivalent of the pure poetry of a Mallarmé, drama in all its dehumanized splendor, cleansed of naturalism. To cleanse itself of its human dimension, the theater of the future must become pure spectacle, pure artifice, amusement, jocularity, mime, pantomime. The key paragraph in this 1921 piece reads as follows:

> Art is not an obligation, but a delightful caprice: no necessity external to the artistic work compels us to go to it. No law of public order imposes on us the task of reading verse, viewing paintings, listening to music, or attending the theater. Neither are we drawn to it by any vital demand, as hunger yoking us to work. If, then, art does not thrive by relying on a necessity external to it, it will have to justify itself to itself for its own sake. This justification can be no more than a single justification: causing pleasure. And each art, in order to exist in its plenitude, in order to be different from the rest, must guarantee a pleasure that only it can give. In this way each one of the arts acquires internal justification, becoming necessary, absolutely necessary, for the engenderment of a determined pleasure. The theater of the present is, for a select public, clearly unnecessary, because the pleasure it proffers can be obtained with less risk and effort through reading. The result: theater is today the fifth wheel of a cart (321).

Once again, a few years before he composed "Dehumanization," Ortega had formulated a theory of art, this time including theater, which clearly anticipated the fundamental esthetic principles of his most influential anti-naturalistic work: art for art's sake, an asocial art whose strict pleasure is the exclusive derivative of its internal structure, owing no allegiance to the external affairs of man at large.

And it is precisely in "Dehumanization" that the ideas on the theater of the second Ortega reach their maximal expression, during a brief, yet key evaluation of Pirandello's Six Characters in Search of an Author, published in the same year that Ortega was speculating on the possibility of pure theater, and seized upon by him as the salient example of dehumanization in the theater, not long after Pirandello's work had achieved international acclaim, among the cognoscenti at least, as an intellectual masterpiece.

After informing us earlier on that one of Pirandello's great social contributions stems from the fact that he forced the masses to abandon all pretensions and recognize themselves for what they really were, "mere ingredient of the social structure, inert matter in the historical process," among other refined definitions,[18] he returns to Pirandello and Six Characters in the chapter of "Dehumanization" titled "A Reverse Turn." In the course of this brief assessment, the Italian dramatist is depicted, much like his contemporaries in painting, as one who "inspires meditation in the aficionado of esthetics of the drama," since Pirandello had succeeded in reversing the tables in the theater from the traditional perception of characters as people to their perception of characters as characters, as concepts or "pure scheme," replacing traditional "pseudopersons who symbolize ideas" with the real thing, "the drama of ideas."

The dehumanizing intent of Six Characters is clear, continues Ortega, and this demonstrates that there are fertile possibilities for the theater of the future, where, happily we may assume, disorientation will reign supreme among an unsophisticated public that does not know how to adjust its vision to an inverted perspective, just as it reigns supreme among a public searching for human drama in a play like Six Characters, a public confused by the fact that Pirandello intentionally suppresses human drama, transforming it into irony by replacing it with theatrical fiction as fiction. The majority, Ortega concludes, is frustrated because it does not realize that it has witnessed a delightful artistic fraud, an art which, like all arts, becomes all the more exquisite in direct proportion to the dominance of its fraudulent texture. Pure theater at its best, we may conclude, incarnate in the genius of Pirandello.

Yet the esthetic pronouncements of "Dehumanization," including Ortega's ideas on the theater, were destined to undergo yet one more significant modification during the philosopher's mature phase, after the publication of Being and Time in 1927 disoriented Ortega to the point where he abandoned his theretofore keen interest in literature as literature, opting instead to treat fiction, poetry, and theater as ancillary instruments in the service of a more compelling ontological phenomenology where the human being himself becomes the primary, supreme historical reality, and where dehumanization itself becomes a thing of the past.[19]

CHAPTER IV

AN ONTOLOGICAL POSTSCRIPT

The publication of the monumental Being and Time by Husserl's foremost disciple in 1927, a year in which Heidegger, who reached beyond his mentor's bracketing of the concrete world in order to describe what it meant to be thrown into this world among its things, was still teaching philosophy at Marburg-where Ortega had learned his most valuable lessons -, was the cause of a great deal of consternation and anxiety which became manifest in Ortega's rather pathetic, retrospective effort to debunk the work of Heidegger, as he attempted, and as his own disciples, notably Julián Marías, subsequently attempted, to demonstrate with subtle hindsight that Ortega indeed predates Heidegger in his radical view of man as history.

Yet notwithstanding the persistent efforts of Ortega and Marías both, Morón Arroyo, whose name I have mentioned frequently during the course of this study, and with good reason, has clearly demonstrated, while at the same time stressing Ortega's originality, especially with respect to his application of Heideggerian methodology to history and sociology, that Heidegger, not Ortega, was indeed the founder of existential phenomenology.[1]

In any case, the anxiety caused by the publication of Being and Time motivated Ortega to a position where his overriding concern with an anthropocentric view of history, together with his frenetic scramble to document his own originality in this respect, left him but little time and interest to indulge in extraphilosophical matters as he had repeatedly indulged in them during the first three decades of his evolution as philosopher.

His new interest in a phenomenology which was exclusively ontological eclipsed his secondary interests to a point where literature became a kind of historical biography, to a point where it became a handmaiden to the drama called man, to a point even where the intrinsic evaluation of a work of art as such no longer fascinated him, as can be documented by his surprising confession, some five years after the publication of "Dehumanization," that new art, being as it is pure artifice, "a libidinous caprice," represented a frivolous "falsification of life."[2] That very same fraud in art which was so appealing to Ortega during the years that he was writing on Proust, Mallarmé, Góngora, Pirandello, as well as on fraudulent painters, became, in itself, meaningless.

Yet this is not equivalent to saying that poetry, theater, Goethe, and Cervantes, among others, where destined to vanish from the work of the mature Ortega, for the fact is that they certainly did not, but were rather consigned a different role as they were made the object of a new type of critical disquisition, one in which Ortega overcame the view of art for its own sake and used works of art to suit his new purpose.

Ortega's first sustained effort on a single author during this new critical direction is a piece on Goethe whose title, "Goethe from Within" (1932),3 provides us with a substantial clue as to its orientation. It is an impressive inquiry into the life of Goethe via Heidegger, although, in addition to the revealing statement that "art is a very respectable entity, but superficial and frivolous when compared to the terrible seriousness of life," it includes a lengthy note in which Ortega denies any debt to Heidegger.4

"Goethe from Within," stuffed with the ontological lexicon of Heidegger, wordy, yet phenomenological to the core, is a summons to a new form of literary biography which would sculpt the object of its attention not in the grandiose, monumental manner of tradition, in which the resulting statue is mere macroscopic bulk, but rather through an "inverse optics," through the microscopic, internal inquiry into the dynamics of existence - as opposed to the dynamics of the work itself, which was Ortega's main target in discussing Proust's microcosm -, the vital structure of a "shipwrecked" Goethe, one who ultimately opted to be unfaithful to his genuine destiny, his vocation, his being per se.

To structure Goethe's biography from this point of view, says Ortega, would teach us a paramount lesson with respect to our own individual existence, since Goethe is among the first to intuit that life is a struggle with individual destiny, human life a becoming of the self, "an absolute and problematic task." And so it is that toward the conclusion of his essay, Ortega offers a distinctly new meaning for classical figures in general, one in which biography in the existential sense of the work and I eclipses all other values of the work. It almost seems, to this reader at least, that the unbridled impressionism of Miguel de Unamuno as this is manifest in his Life of Don Quixote and Sancho, which predates Ortega's inquiry into Goethe by more than twenty-five years, impulsively and arrogantly rejected by him, both prior to and with the publication of Meditations, as well as implicitly until 1927, suddenly became a highly lucrative critical norm:

> What I am affirming is that the
> clarification of the figure Goethe, so that
> it has a more radical meaning, so that it may

serve us, can only be attained by inverting our way of treating him.

> There is only one way to save a classical writer: using him irreverently for our own salvation - that is to say, abstracting his classicism, bringing it to ourselves, contemporizing it, injecting it with a new pulse, with the blood of our veins, whose ingredients are our passions...and our problems. Instead of being centenarians during this centennial, let us attempt the resurrection of a classic by resubmerging him in existence (419).[5]

More than fifteen years later, in such diverse places as Aspen, Hamburg, San Sebastián and Madrid, Ortega gave a series of guest lectures in celebration of Goethe's bicentennial which are in essence a re-elaboration of the fundamental ideas previously set forth in "Goethe from Within," in addition to the fact that these individual lectures themselves overlap excessively. For these reasons, I shall discuss them only briefly, and as a unit.[6]

The principal thrust of these lectures, as was the case with the 1932 essay, is their plea for a new Goethe, the one who transcended traditional cultural naturalism to sense the drama of being and becoming as no one else in the history of Western literature: as opposed to the Goethe of traditional erudition-the macroscopic titan, we might say, referring back to Ortega's earlier piece on Goethe -, the cold statue bereft of any ontological dimensions, the intimate Goethe who understood that human life was not factum but rather faciendum, despite the fact that Ortega makes sarcastic reference to European existentialism in his Hamburg lecture.[7]

It becomes abundantly clear that our mature philosopher returned to his earlier interest in man with a vengeance, with the difference that he too, like the Goethe he portrays, had transcended classical naturalism in favor of radical individualism.

Literature as a kind of dictionary which elucidates existence is also the central theme of "The Idea of Theater," a lecture delivered in Lisbon in 1946.[8]

After pointedly reminding his audience that the humans painted by Velázquez were men, and that Alexander too was a man, as a prelude to his inquiry into theater as human phenomenon, Ortega resorts to the familiar phenomenological lexicon which stretches all the way back to Meditations to inform his listeners

71

of the concealed or latent structures lurking beneath the surface of things whose truth must be uncovered, or dis-covered, in order for these structures to become manifest.

One such truth is the truth of the theater, a structure so intimately related to human life as to cause Ortega to approach its truth in terms of an ontological dialectic which occupies the greater part of his essay. During this dialectic, dramatists, players and audience collaborate in what is ultimately a diversion, a farse which is a necessary parenthesis from the overwhelming seriousness of being, a distraction from life as constant struggle, an unreal metaphor whose purpose is relief from care and anxiety. In a passage which is probably the most frequently quoted of Ortega's descriptions of life, he has the following to say:

> Life is not something just there, like a thing, but rather always something to be done, a task, a gerund, a faciendum. And yet, if what we have to do each moment were given us already decided, the task of living would be less grueling. But there is no such thing; at every moment there open to us diverse possibilities of action, and we have no choice but to select one, to decide in this moment what we are going to do in the next, subject to our unique and non-transferable responsibility (467).

It is because of the necessity of relief from this awesome burden, in the form of a pause, that we leave the house for the theater, which, quite understandably, is now no longer just written literature as it was in 1921, in "In Praise of The Bat," when we could simply stay at home and reap the rewards of Hamlet in isolation. On the contrary, theater in 1946 is everything that literature is not, according to Ortega. Due to its urgent vital role as relief, the conception of theater as literary genre, as mere words, prose or verse, is a serious misconception, for it is now of utmost importance that we participate by hearing, especially by seeing, by witnessing a spectacle as spectacle, as opposed to a secondary immersion into its pages. During the course of this depiction of theater as a visual art, Ortega, in direct contradiction to what he had said in 1921, says, among other things, that "dramaturgy is only secondarily and partially a literary genre, and, consequently, even that portion of it which is truly literature cannot be contemplated separately from what theater as spectacle is."[9]

A 1952 prologue to the Spanish edition of the book-length Arabic love poem by Ibn Hazm[10] provides further, parallel evidence, of the post-1927 change in Ortega's approach to literature, for the prologue in question is totally devoid not only of any first-phase criteria for judging poetry, but devoid as well of the slightest inclination to approach the poem as poetry, the poem as its metaphor, or as its structure.

Ortega's essay can be adequately described as a historical inquiry into the human meaning of love in medieval Arabic communities, and its historical relationship to European courtly love in general.

Its main thrust is that the concept of love, an anthropological phenomenon - books are actions by men, Ortega stresses -, evolves historically, and that consequently, the critic approaching a book such as The Dove's Necklace should do so through an historico-philological perspective, treating medieval Arab communities in Spain as distinct communities, as opposed to treating them as Hispano-Semitic cultures, an apparent allusion to the controversial theories of Américo Castro, especially as these theories are set forth in The Historical Reality of Spain (first published in 1948), in which Castro emphasizes the Semitic origin of Spanish culture. Whichever the more valid historiographical approach may be, the point is that in this essay Ortega strays into areas which he had consciously, scrupulously avoided during his phenomeno-structuralist formal period as critic, now consciously eschewing what had by 1952 become the defunct glories of metaphorical bliss.

Some comment on "What is Reading?", already discussed extensively by M. Arroyo,[11] may serve as concluding commentary on individual pieces by Ortega related to criticism, as well as a preface to a summary statement evaluating some five decades of sporadic practical criticism by one of the foremost thinkers of our times, and an attempt to locate this criticism somewhere within the contemporary critical landscape.

"What is Reading?", published posthumously, is the preface to what was projected as a lengthy meditation on Plato's Symposium, conceived around 1946, yet never completed.

This preface may be viewed as a refinement of previous references to reading as these appear in such diverse places as Ortega's second essay on Baroja, in "Ideas on the Novel," and in a complement to "What is Reading?", the 1935 fragment "What is a Book?", in which Ortega describes a book as a "tremendous human reality," and treats reading as printed discourse that must be completed through the hard efforts of a thinking reader, with reference once again to Plato.[12]

"What is Reading?", which posits reading as a highly problematic human activity, begins with the statement that reading a book, along with other human activity, is a "utopian task," since the initial task can never really be fully consummated.

This is true, on the one hand, because all discourse is deficient, communicating less than is its intention, while on the other hand, paradoxically enough, all discourse is "exuberant," laden with the enormous inarticulated possibilities which the active reader - the genuine reader - must extrapolate from "the mental reality unstated" in this discourse. To read in earnest, Ortega informs us, is to read the actual text against the background of its "total latent interior," the only way to at least approximate true meaning. Thus, reading is a highly complicated task, an enormous responsibility, for it implies, among other things, that the reader must know more than the author himself knew, according to Ortega, who, in paraphrasing Kant's remarks on reading Plato, is in total agreement with the German philosopher that reading Plato implies understanding Plato better than he understood himself (752).

While all this is an apparent throwback to what Ortega had already stated or implied between 1913 and 1927, as well as being an obvious throwback to the methodology actually applied by him during the course of his brilliant sallies into the unstated realms of Azorín, Baroja and Dostoyevsky, in order to "complete" their meaning, "What is Reading?" nonetheless incorporates a stricter linguistic dimension which was absent from Ortega's earlier hermeneutics, thus bringing his work closer to the more recent semiological mainstream of structuralist critical inquiry.

The problematic human activity known as reading is now additionally compounded because the "completion," or "salvation" of an author - a term used repeatedly by Ortega in Meditations- is further complicated by the inherent imperfection of written language, a discourse whose form is deprived of its primogenital dimension of modulation, facial gesture, manual and somatic gesticulation, which are essential appendices to its meaning. This is so because the spoken - "heard" - language precedes its written form, which in turn means that its sound, and phonological nuances in particular, are central to, inherent in, its meaning. And preceding the "heard" or spoken form of discourse is the problem of articulation per se: the biological, strictly muscular activity of larynx, mouth, nose, are also factors which must be taken into account.

Authentic discourse, then, is the result of a vital reaction to a specific physical circumstance. Primarily gesture, it is much more complete than the "petrified," fixed discourse found in books (762).

The conclusion of Ortega's prologue, after he once again stresses the inherent deficiency of a book, which he nevertheless considers to be the only form in which we can state certain things, reads as follows:

> Now a book is for us the absence of its author, and written discourse a residue of what preceded its author. We have a statement without an author. Why do we emphasize this so? Isn't it an exaggeration to lend so much importance to the gesticulatory pattern in which a word is first conceived?...It is beyond dispute that if we were able to behold Plato in the flesh, just seeing him and hearing him articulate would be adequate for the true resolution of the grandiose problems which the reading of his books posit, and without this, they will probably remain perpetually enigmatic.

What becomes clear is that the completion of Ortega's reflections on Plato would have entailed a substantial ontological confrontation with the world of signs.

We can now proceed to formulate a synoptic assessment of the results of some fifty years of reading by one of the most astute of contemporary European readers.

From the normative classicism of his early period, in which the breaching of traditional ethical naturalism was tantamount to a sacrilegious transgression, Ortega was thrust, perhaps caught up in the tide, as he himself seems to indicate, into the overlapping world of formalism, semiotic patterns, structuralism, and subsequently, phenomenological ontology, all of whose roots seem ultimately traceable to Husserl's "rigorous new science,"[13] perhaps a "stroke of good fortune," as Ortega described it.

His normative period to one side, in Ortega's reading of Azorín, Baroja, Proust, Stendhal, and Dostoyevsky, we can clearly discern that he predated the poetics of prominent members of the Geneva School such as Roman Ingarden, whose Literary Work of Art dates from 1931, and the younger J. Hillis Miller, whose Charles Dickens was published in 1959, as we can additionally discern through these same readings that Ortega had at least anticipated the 1921 "literariness" of a Jakobson and, subsequently, the other more linguistically-oriented, Parisian counterparts of the Geneva School, finally reaching a point in "What is Reading?"

where he himself began to delve into the formal patterns of sounds and words, falling somewhat short, however, of the post-structuralist openness of "unlimited significations."[14]

With respect to Ortega's reflections on the novel per se, it might prove worthwhile to attempt to clarify these in the context of their modernity by looking at them against the background of the theoretical work of the eminently phenomenological Robbe-Grillet, for we can reasonably conclude, and with adequate confidence, that the theoretical framework of the practitioners of the nouveau roman was all laid out for these advocates of "the privileged sense of sight" by Ortega between 1913 and 1924, the latter being the date of their maximal elaboration, much prior to their heralded translation into a radically new fictional form. To a large extent, it can even be said that Ortega had thoroughly intuited the coming of this new novel, although not precisely the form in which it actually became manifest.

Even a rapid reading of Robbe-Grillet's For a New Novel[15] may serve as sufficient confirmation of the clear affinity between the French novelist and the author of "Dehumanization" and "Ideas On the Novel."

In his strict formalism - a term which is not especially palatable to him -, in his insistence that the novelist owes exclusive allegiance to literature and nothing else, in his derisive treatment of Balzacian fiction, in his virulent opposition to the novel as human passion - his rabid opposition to the social novel in particular -, in his general denouncement of the nineteenth century forms which he claims have become stagnant, in his prouncement that these forms have indeed died, thereby compelling the genuine novelist to a new form, in his emphasis on "presence" and "the visual adjective," all in a general effort to sever the novel from its traditional human contingency, in sum, in his effort to "dehumanize" the novel, as well as in his prognosticating a problematic future for the novel, among many other things, Robbe-Grillet sounds very much like the Ortega of 1924. So much so that, as was the case with the striking similarity between the trenchant oratory of Clive Bell and the thought of Ortega, to choose just one representative passage from Robbe-Grillet's disquisition on the novel as an illustration of his proximity to Ortega is difficult. The fact is that any one of many may serve this purpose, although I have decided on the following:

> We know that the whole literature of the novel was based on these myths, and on them alone. The writer's traditional role consisted in excavating Nature, in burrowing deeper and deeper to reach some ever more

intimate strata, in finally unearthing some
fragment of a disconcerting secret. Having
descended into the abyss of human passions,
he would send to the seemingly tranquil world
(the world on the surface) triumphant
messages describing the mysteries he had
actually touched with his own hands (23-4).

The obvious accomplishments on the part of Ortega as reader
to one side, we might now pose some questions as to their
significance, as a conclusion to these observations: What do
these accomplishments mean within the contemporary scope of
critical meaning, beyond their meaning as critical achievements?

To cite, as an example, the case of Dostoyevsky as "seen" by
Ortega, which in turn can be related to recent post-structural
directions, is it really valid to conclude that Dostoyevsky is
nothing beyond his craft as novelist? Nothing beyond his
structuring of fiction, and the critical structuration of him?

This view, which seems to have gained so many converts in
recent years, yet which at this date is being increasingly
challenged by a more humanistically-oriented vanguard of
opponents of post-structuralist extremes, by prominent names such
as M. H. Abrams, Walter Reed, and Terry Eagleton (whose book
comes fresh off the press as I am writing this conclusion),[16]
does not seem to be an adequate view. Surely, whatever else he
may be, Dostoyevsky is also his Grand Inquisitor, his insatiable
Father Karamozov, the gambler portrayed by him in a book bearing
the same title, the innocent Myshkin inspired in his reading of
Cervantes, the anguished existentialist of Notes from
Underground, and so forth. This would still be true even should
we decide to deconstruct this defenseless epileptic, this "great
Slav," as Ortega describes him.

For that matter, to cite one more example, one far removed
from Ortega's "hermetism," as well as from his hermetic
haughtiness, are the modern Brazilian naturalism of the Northeast
School of fiction and the school itself really dead? Hardly, for
it seems that these Brazilian novelists have not yet discovered
the time necessary to luxuriate in abstruse parafictional - as
well as parasocial - verbal and cerebral heroics. This
indisputable phenomenon, the phenomenon of compelling, resilient
vitality through an apparently anachronistic form - "present," so
that all men may "see" it - may serve at least as a partial
answer to the angry young post-structuralists, as well as an
answer to Ortega, who, despite himself even, might have focused
his unquestionable genius a bit more toward the center of the
overwhelming problems confronting the human community at large.

REFERENCES

NOTES TO CHAPTER ONE

[1] Ciriaco Morón Arroyo, El sistema de Ortega y Gasset (Madrid, 1968), pp. 77-81.

[2] On the young Ortega's formative years in Marburg and Neo-Kantianism see Philip W. Silver, Ortega as Phenomenologist: The Genesis of Meditations on Quixote (New York, 1978), pp. 15-46; M. Arroyo, ibid., et passim, and Julián Marías, Jose Ortega y Gasset: Circumstance and Vocation (Norman, 1970), pp. 191-206, passim.

A readable translation of Scheler's important work on ethics is the one by Manfred S. Frings and Fung, Roger, Formalism in Ethics and Non-Formal Ethics of Values (Evanston, 1973). In his preface to the third edition of this book (XXXIII) Scheler himself singles out Ortega as the Spaniard who followed both his value theory and his sociological thought, with reference to specific essays by Ortega. For one reason or another, as M. Arroyo has pointed out (26-9), Julián Marías seems to have tried to suppress any mention of Scheler in his studies on Ortega. M. Arroyo repeatedly mentions Scheler as a decisive influence in his own definitive study.

On Ortega's ethics in general, see the brief, incisive overview by José Luis Aranguren, La ética de Ortega (Madrid, 1953).

To date, the most important longer study of Ortega's phenomenology is the pioneering study by Silver, op. cit., while the few pages devoted to this same topic by M. Arroyo are a model of analytic clarity (206-15). See also on Ortega as phenomenologist the renowned historian of phenomenology Herbert Spiegelberg, The Phenomenological Movement: A Historical Introduction (The Hague, 1960), II, pp. 611-22. Spiegelberg stresses the fact that it was the young Ortega who singlehandedly was responsible for the widespread popularity of phenomenology both in Spain and Latin America, where it has become "one of the dominant philosophies." Spiegelberg also discusses Ortega's debt, and objections to, both Husserl and Scheler. His concluding chapter (II, 653-701) is one of the clearest introductions to the fundamentals of the phenomenological method.

With respect to the application of phenomenology to literary criticism, the recent book by Robert R. Magliola, Phenomenology and Literature (West Lafayette, 1977) is an indispensable introduction, notwithstanding the fact that Magliola makes no mention of Ortega in his excellent study.

3 Azorín, Obras completas (Madrid, 1959), Vol. II, pp. 433-6.

4 El arte desde el punto de vista sociológico (trans. Ricardo Rubio, 1902).

5 José Ortega y Gasset, Obras completas (Madrid, 1946-69). See Vol. III, p. 353 of this eleven volume edition. Subsequent references by volume and page number will appear mostly in the text.

All translations from Ortega's work, including titles, are my own.

6 I, 13-62.

7 I shall return to this essay in the third chapter of this study.

8 For a typical early defense of socialism see X, 86-90; 139-42, passim. The 1910 lecture titled "Social Pedagogy as Political Program" (I, 503-21) is directly indebted to the writings of Natorp (Marías, 215-16).

9 On Unamuno's early esthetics and the concept of intrahistory see, e.g., my study Unamuno and the Novel (University of North Carolina, 1974), pp. 14-29. M. Arroyo has also pointed to the Unamuno imprint on "Maxims" (364-5; 371). On Ortega's relations with Unamuno, see Marías, 132-45.

10 I, 64.

11 196-7. For an additional, earlier (1907) defense of classicism, see the same article in which Ortega begins to censure Unamuno, "On Classical Studies" (I, 63-7), where Ortega equates culture with what is "human," insisting on the traditional, classical role of science, ethics, and esthetics as the means toward civilization.

12 M. Arroyo, p. 77. José Ferrater Mora, in Ortega y Gasset: An Outline of his Philosophy (New Haven, 1957), p. 6, refers to this same period as Ortega's objectivist period.

13 IX, 477-500 should be read in conjunction with II, 103-125.

[14] On this aspect of Baroja's essay, see the article by M. Arroyo, "Ortega y Gasset: Práctica y teoría de la lectura" in Homenaje a J. López Morillas (Madrid, 1982), p. 294.

[15] See I, 261-3.

[16] In X, 51-5 and 95-9 respectively.

[17] Scheler is mentioned frequently throughout Ortega's works. See e.g. "Max Scheler, Inebriate of Essences," in IV, 507-510: "the thinker par excellence of our generation." (510).

[18] I, 238-43.

[19] See this critical masterpiece in II, 157-91.

[20] In "Dehumanization" (III, 360-364).

NOTES TO CHAPTER TWO

[1] Published in 1934 (VIII, 15-58).

[2] M. Arroyo (211-13) disagrees with Ortega's prouncement that phenomenology was incapable of system, stressing that Heidegger founded a whole new system based on a slightly modified phenomenology. Even Ortega's subsequent objections to Husserl's bracketing and intentionality are taken to task by M. Arroyo (213), while with respect to the contention on the part of Ortega's loyal disciple J. Marías that his mentor had gone much beyond Husserl in his well-known piece "An Essay on Esthetics by Way of a Prologue" (1914), M. Arroyo also documents that this is simply not so, restricting the importance of Ortega's "executive I" to art (214-15).

[3] See M. Arroyo, 73-81; 133-41; 208-12 passim. Silver (86-7) disagrees with M. Arroyo's contention that Ortega had never really pre-empted Heidegger's systematic ontology, finding that Meditations was "indeed pre-emptive of Heidegger's notion of Being-in-the-World." In this respect, Silver is in agreement with Marías (435-7), and coincides even with Spiegelberg, who, not having had the advantage provided by Arroyo's study, seems to have based his conclusions on Ortega's indebtedness both to Husserl and Heidegger entirely on what Ortega himself says of these two indelible influences (Spiegelberg, II, 615-16).

In passing, it is noteworthy that all of Ortega's objections to Husserl seem to have been articulated in retrospect, after he had read Heidegger's <u>Being and Time</u>. I shall return to this problem in the concluding chapter of this study.

[4] Reprinted in Silver (ed. and trans.), <u>Phenomenology and Art</u> (New York, 1975).

[5] I, 244-61.

[6] Further evidence of Ortega's interest in phenomenology around this same time can be seen, among other places, in "Consciousness, Object, and Its Three Dimensions" (1915, II, 61-6) and in "Esthetics on the Streetcar" (1916, II, 33-9), one of the clearest examples of the practical application of phenomenology to esthetics.

[7] By M. Arroyo (381-2) in his discussion of Ortega's <u>Meditations</u>.

[8] I, 318: "These <u>Meditations</u>, free from erudition..., are inspired by philosophical desires. However, I would be indebted to the reader if he were to undertake their reading without too many demands. They are not philosophy, which is science. They are simply essays. And an essay is science minus the explicit proof. For the writer it is a question of intellectual honor not to write anything subject to proof without possessing it beforehand. But it is also necessary for him to eliminate from his work all apodictic appearances, leaving the documentation merely implicit in ellipse, so that he who needs it may find it, and so that it does not impede, on the other hand, the growth of the intimate warmth with which these ideas were thought. Even books whose purpose is exclusively scientific are beginning to be written in a less didactic style..."

[9] It is quite possible that both the form and content of Ortega's preface owe a substantial debt to the chapter from Husserl's <u>Ideas</u> titled "The Thesis of the Natural Standpoint and Its Suspension," whose first section is titled "The World of the Natural Standpoint: I and My World About Me": "I am aware of a world, spread out in space endlessly...I discover it immediately, intuitively, I experience it. Through touch, sight, hearing, etc., in the different ways of sensory perception, corporeal things...are for me simply there...whether or not I pay them special attention...by considering, thinking, feeling, willing. I can let my attention wander from the writing table...through the unseen portions of the room...to the verandah, into the garden...and so forth...to the objects I precisely know...a knowledge which...first changes into clear intuiting with the bestowal of attention..." (Trans. W. R. Gibson, 3rd ed., London, 1953, pp. 100-02).

[10] "Sexual pleasure seems to consist of a sudden discharge of nervous energy. Esthetic fruition is a sudden discharge of allusive emotions. By analogy, philosophy is a sudden discharge of intellection" (317).

[11] Robert Magliola, op. cit., p. 63.

[12] "I see in criticism a zealous effort to potentiate a given work...Criticism is not biography, nor is it justified as independent labor, if it does not propose the completion of a work. This means that criticism must be a work that introduces all those sentimental and ideological tools thanks to which the average reader can experience the clearest and most intense impression possible in a work. The procedure is the orientation of criticism toward an affirmative meaning, addressing it not to the correction of the author, but to endowing the reader with a more perfect visual organ. A work is completed through the completion of its reading" (321).

[13] The Spanish critics Juan Valera and Menéndez Pelayo, the latter a giant in his times, as was Sainte-Beuve in his, are treated similarly in Meditations, since they lack perspective and applaud mediocrity (339).

[14] The "absurd existence" is an obvious reference to Unamuno's brilliant impressionistic masterpiece The Life of Don Quixote and Sancho (1905).

[15] Magliola (49) traces the hermeneutical circle to Schleiermacher, on whom Ortega also elaborates in Meditations (339), although in other terms.

[16] The criticism of Spain culminates in Invertebrate Spain (1921).

[17] "Here of course we have the beginning of what would later be called, improperly, realism, and which, strictly speaking, should be called impressionism. For twenty centuries the Mediterraneans enrolled their artists under this banner of impressionistic art: sometimes exclusively, at times tacitly and partially, the will toward the sensual as such always triumphed. For the Greek, what we see is governed and modified by thinking and only has value in accordance as it ascends to an ideal symbol. For us, this ascension is rather a descent: sensualism bursts the chains of enslavement to ideas and declares its independence. The Mediterranean is a perpetual, ardent justification of sensualism, of appearance, of surfaces, of fleeting impressions..." (347).

[18] See especially the chapter "The Panther or Sensualism" (346-9). Ortega, while he never mentions phenomenology in Meditations, consistently alludes to it throughout his book.

[19] Husserl discusses reduction in the first chapter of the second part of Ideas (1913). For the purpose of this study I have made use of the standard English translation by W. R. Boyce (op. cit.). See on reduction pp. 101-11 of this edition.

Brief, clear expositions on Husserlian reduction can be seen in E. Parl Welch, The Philosophy of Edmund Husserl (New York, 1941), pp. 141-61; Marvin Farber, The Aims of Phenomenology (New York, 1966), pp. 55-62; Joseph Kockelmans, A First Introduction to Husserl's Phenomenology (Dusquesne, 1967), pp. 133-64, and Kockelmans (op. cit.), which contains pieces on reduction by prominent phenomenologists, including Kockelmans, Richard Schmitt, Emmanuel Levinas.

A brief, exceptionally lucid explanation of the application of Husserlain reduction to literary criticism appears in Magliola (38-9).

[20] A primary example of this same sort occurs during Ortega's inquiry into the cultural phenomenon known as beauty in "Esthetics on the Streetcar" (op. cit., 1916), where Ortega extends the imperfect or incomplete line of a female nose which is the object of his attention, carrying it to its completion as part of a model for beauty. He then extends this method to include its practical application to ethics as well.

[21] Flaubert's acknowledged debt to Cervantes is cited as an outstanding example (398).

[22] The diminishing appeal of the contemporary novel is attributed by Ortega to a minimal presence of poetic dynamism, the weakness in the tension between the real and the ideal. "For this reason we can predict that the novel of the nineteenth century will soon be unreadable: it contains the least amount of poetic dynamism" (399).

Similar, although more refined statements on the demise of the novel appear ten years later in "Ideas on the Novel" (III, 387-90).

[23] II, 69-102.

[24] See Magliola's chapter "The Geneva School and Its Accomplices" (19-56), wherein the author analyzes the school's application of Husserlian phenomenology to practical criticism,

with extensive reference to figures such as Marcel Raymond, George Poulet, J. Hillis Miller, among others.

M. H. Abrams, A Glossary of Literary Terms (4th ed., New York, 1981), pp. 133-5, contains a concise history of the Geneva School of literary criticism, as well as a long list of selected studies by and on individual figures prominent in the school. See especially Sarah Lawall, Critics of Consciousness (Harvard, 1968).

[25] M. Arroyo discusses Ortega's commentary on Baroja in the context of theory and practice of reading in his article "Ortega y Gasset: Práctica y teoría de la lectura" (see n. 14, Chapter 1) where, among other things, he mentions the hermeneutic circle and states that "Reading or criticism has as its function the discovery of coordinates, that is to say, what Ortega calls the unarticulated mental reality, present in the text." I shall return to this article in my final chapter.

[26] I, 403-6.

[27] In this same article, in a similar inquiry into El Greco's baroque dynamism, we discover a reversal of the crude treatment of El Greco found in Ortega's pre-perspectivist work, especially, e.g., in "Renan" (1909), where an immature eye abuses the painter for his verisimilitude, among other things (I, 451-3).

[28] III, 399-403.

[29] Further comment of any significance on Dostoyevsky can be seen in the 1927 essay "Questions on the Novel" (III, 568-73), where, in addition to discussing the Catholic esthetics of Henri Massis and Francois Mauriac, Ortega contrasts the impoverished, schematic coherence of Balzac with the fertile "incongruency" which the French novel inherited from Dostoyevsky (573).

[30] Further reference to the dullness of Balzac appears in Ortega's chapter on Dostoyevsky and Proust: "For the novel, as opposed to other poetic genres, demands that we not perceive it as a novel, that we not see its curtain and stage lights. Balzac, read today, awakes us from our novelistic dream with every page, for we constantly collide with his novelistic scaffolding" (402).

[31] Of course, this would also include the absence of the social and political world, too closely related to the real world, which we must forget. A portion of "Hermetism" stands as an emphatic illustration of the enormous change that took place in Ortega's critical and esthetic values between 1902-1924: "A

purely esthetic need imposes hermetism, the force of an orbit sealed off from any effective reality, on the novel. And this circumstance, brings about the result, among many others, that the novel cannot aspire directly to being philosophy, a political pamphlet, a sociological study, a moral tract. It can be no more than a novel, <u>its interior cannot in itself transcend to anything exterior</u>, as the dream would cease the moment we try to stretch our arm from our alert position in order to grasp a real object and introduce it into the magical sphere of which we are dreaming" (412).

[32] II, 701-9.

[33] An apparent analogy to the "bracketing out" of all other things in the natural world (704).

[34] VII, 132-3. Ortega renders <u>Du côté de chez Swann</u> and its counterpart as "Por el lado de Swann" and "Del lado de los Guermantes" respectively, neither of which helps solve the problem of the exact rendition of these titles into English. If we choose the rendition "Swann's Perspective" and the "Guermantian Perspective," we at least approximate the meaning that Ortega finds in these titles.

[35] These early references to Stendhal can be seen in I, 22; 112 and 114 respectively.

[36] II, 178.

[37] II, 402; 408.

[38] V, 563-96. Similarly, a 1916 piece ostensibly on Benjamin Constant's <u>Adolphe</u> really uses this brief novel as a pretext for a disquisition into love, as well as into romanticism and classicism (II, 25-8).

For further comment of interest on Stendhal, see II, 706 and III, 549, both of which references deal with characterization.

In his 1923 essay "What Are Values?", Ortega refers to Stendhal, along with Dostoyevsky, Cervantes, Goya, Michelangelo, as part of a group of impractically oriented seers who nevertheless discovered "values previously latent in the universe" (VI, 335).

[39] II, 229-34.

[40] In 1932 Ortega refers to Anatole France as a gifted writer who nevertheless lacked "the fertile imagination of a

novelist." Consequently, France's characters are mostly a replica of one another (IV, 390).

41 III, 544-50.

42 See Clive Bell, Art (London, 1949, new ed.) pp. 70-71. On the art of the nineteenth century, Bell is in perfect agreement with Ortega: "It is the general acceptance of this view - that the accurate imitation of objects is an essential quality in a work of art - and the general inability to create, or even recognize, aesthetic qualities, that mark the nineteenth century as the end of a slope. Except stray artists and odd amateurs, and you may say that in the middle of the nineteenth century art had ceased to exist" (192).

For choice comments on the gross herd, see pp. 25, 39, 65 passim.

43 The most important phenomenological polemic against naturalism is Husserl's "Philosophy as Rigorous Science" (1911), an excellent English edition of which, together with a clear introduction and extremely useful notes, appears in Quentin Lauer, Phenomenology and the Crisis of Philosophy (N.Y., 1965).

44 M. Arroyo (El sistema, 375-9) relates the concept of dehumanization to the idea of art as sport or game, as well as to the type of anthropocentric biologism or vitalism which characterizes Ortega's thought between 1920 and 1927, culminating in the well-known essay "The Theme of Our Time" (1926). Ortega's pronouncements on art as game and its relationship to primitive vitalism are traced by M. Arroyo to the works of Simmel and Spengler.

A typical statement from the period in question extolling the role of the "impractical" in culture is the following (1920): "If we understand work as that effort imposed by necessity and dictated by utility, then I maintain that whatever is worth anything on this earth is not a product of work. On the contrary, it was born as a spontaneous efflorescence of the superfluous and disinterested effort in which all plethoric nature usually seeks recreation. Culture is not the offspring of work, but of sport...the superior form of human existence is sports. Some day I shall try to explain why I have arrived at this conclusion, demonstrating how social progress, and new scientific discoveries...anticipate a historical turn toward a sportive and festive idea of life" (II, 302).

For more on the play theory of art see Melvin M. Rader, A Modern Book of Esthetics (N.Y. 1935), pp. 3-52. Rader, in an introductory note to essays by Konrad Lange and Karl Groos traces the initial equation of art to play to Kant (<u>The Critique of Judgment</u>, 1790), and its most important early elaboration to Schiller (<u>Letters on the Aesthetic Education of Man</u>, 1795).

[45] Abrams, <u>op</u>. <u>cit</u>. (165-7) contains a concise history of Russian formalism and its affinity with American New Criticism, with emphasis on the concept of literariness and figures such as Roman Jakobson, Vladimir Propp, Tzvetan Todorov.

See also Magliola (84-90, <u>passim</u>) and Jonathan Culler, <u>Structuralist Poetics</u> (Ithaca, 1975), pp. 189-240, <u>passim</u>.

A useful, clear English edition of Todorov, a leading figure in contemporary structuralism, is his <u>Introduction to Poetics</u> (Minneapolis, 1981).

NOTES TO CHAPTER THREE

[1] I, 570-4.

[2] M. Arroyo (371) has pointed out that <u>spiraculum vitae</u> has little to do with German mysticism.

[3] I, 26-7.

[4] I, 113.

[5] In the essay on Antonio Machado, I, 571.

[6] I, 129.

[7] On mysticism in general see, e.g., in <u>What is Philosophy?</u> (1929) Chapter V, "In Defense of the Theologian as Opposed to the Mystic" (VII, 329-43). On Santa Teresa see, e.g., I, 444.

[8] I, 443-67.

[9] On this same essay and its disdain for metaphor see M. Arroyo, p. 387.

[10] III, 13-24. A complete English edition of Tagore, <u>Collected Poems and Plays</u> was published in 1966.

[11] <u>Les Forces éternelles</u> (Paris, 1923).

[12] IV, 481-4.

[13] See III, 372.

[14] III, 580-6.

[15] For the 1914 and 1924 texts on metaphor see VI, 256-61 and II, 387-400. On this same topic see M. Arroyo, 387-91.

[16] I, 522-6.

[17] See "In Praise of The Bat" (III, 319-27).

[18] III, 355.

[19] The chapter in "Ideas" titled "Two Theaters" (III, 395-8), in which Ortega contrasts the more conceptual French classical drama with the demotic color and action of the Spanish drama, especially as this is manifest in the brilliant spontaneity of the dramatist Lope de Vega, has only a marginal relationship to the ideas on theater expressed in "In Praise of The Bat" and in "Dehumanization," although, rather unexpectedly, Ortega concludes this chapter with some rather favorable remarks on the Spanish theater of the Golden Age.

Don Juan is also discussed during this second phase as psychological symbol, not so much in the context of any specific drama as art, but rather in the context of the individual, "Don Juan as the authentic and maximum Sevillian," who is not really a sensual egotist, but rather a genuine hero, according to Ortega. See VI, 121-37 (1921).

NOTES TO CHAPTER FOUR

[1] M. Arroyo's rebuttal includes a marvelously concise inquiry into the meaning of Heidegger's work, including its relationship to the phenomenology of Husserl. See especially pp. 134-41; 158-68, passim.

Other notably brief, concise, clear accounts on phenomenological ontology include those by Calvin O. Schrag in Kockelmans (ed., op. cit., pp. 277-93), which is followed by a clear translation of significant portions of Heidegger's work; Magliola (57-80; 174-91), who also includes the application of Heidegger to literary criticism. A longer exposition on Heidegger and related problems, also a rare model of clarity, appears in Spiegelberg (I, 271-357).

With respect to Ortega's inordinate reaction to Heidegger, see, e.g., in his lengthy study of Leibniz (VIII, 13-358), the numerous derogatory references to the German philosopher, especially pp. 271-84, and the numerous, lengthy notes to these pages, in one of which Ortega claims to have surpassed Husserl's phenomenological reductionism prior to Heidegger.

2 V, 272.

3 IV, 395-418.

4 "In the admirable book by Heidegger titled _Being and Time_, published in 1927, the author arrives at a definition of life which approximates mine. I cannot say what the proximity between Heidegger's philosophy and the one which has always inspired my writing is, among other reasons, because Heidegger's work is still incomplete, and, on the other hand, my thinking is not adequately developed in _printed_ form; yet I must declare that my debt to this author is very slight. There are barely one or two important concepts in Heidegger which may not pre-exist, at times with a thirteen year advantage, in my books," etc. (403-4).

5 Similar ideas are articulated in "Goethe, the Liberator," a prelude to the longer essay, published in the same year (IV, 421-7).

6 The lectures can be seen in IX, 551-612.

7 With respect to the reference to existentialism, see p. 566: "Some groups of European writers, less numerous than they are noisy, nowadays purport to have man retrogress to nothingness and to leave him transfixed there. There is a great deal to be said about this explosion of nihilistic inspiration which calls itself existentialism. This is not the moment to do so."

8 Together with two supplements, the lecture appears in VII, 441-501.

9 P. 456. Cervantes is assigned a prominent role in "Idea of the Theater" through the famous theatrical episode involving Don Quixote as spectator of Maese Pedro's puppet show, used by Ortega as an illustration of the reality we are and the real ability of theater to carry us along in its unreal magic (462-3).

The appendix to "Idea of the Theater" titled "Masks" (472-96), in which we find mention of a "melodramatic Mr. Heidegger" (496), is both historical and ontological in its focus, and explains Dionysian abandon in similar terms of the need for diversion, the need for human relief from life's oppressive toil.

A curious digression with respect to theater is Ortega's 1935 essay on the melodramatic Zorrilla's _Don Juan_, "The Strangling of Don Juan" (V, 242-50), in which Ortega once again chides performers for their poor presentation as he had done in his youth in "Shylock," although without the same social overtones. In the 1935 piece on <u>Don Juan</u> Ortega additionally defends Zorilla's play in terms of popular tradition. One can only imagine what he would have said about this kind of theater had he chose to comment on it extensively during his Neo-Kantian period.

[10] VII, 41-55.

[11] See Ortega's essay in IX, 751-66 and note 25 to the second chapter of this study.

[12] In "The Mission of a Librarian," V, 230-4.

[13] In his brief, incisive overview, "Phenomenology and Structuralism" (<u>The Human Context</u>, V, Spring 1973, pp. 35-41), Jonathan Culler, using the incomplete projections of Merlau-Ponty as a point of departure, makes an admirable case for placing structuralism where it belongs, within its broader phenomenological context. Culler, in arguing against the perception of structuralism and phenomenology as contrapositions, succeeds in overcoming the dualism of subject and object, stressing the "operative intentionality immanent in the phenomenal world," concluding that "to relate structuralism to phenomenology is simply a way of making an elementary methodological point about structural analysis, a point which, once enunciated, seems obvious but which is too often ignored: if structural analysis is to make sense as an intellectual enterprise it must specify clearly what are the facts about human experience which it attempts to explicate."

The historical indebtedness of structuralism and semiology to Husserlian phenomenology can be documented through reference to Victor Erlich's <u>Russian Formalism: History - Doctrine</u> (The Hague, 1969), in which the author outlines the genesis of the Moscow Linguistic Circle in the context of its indebtedness to Husserl's <u>Logical Investigations</u> (1900), which for the unorthodox linguists "became virtually a Bible" (p. 62). Erlich attributes this huge impact of Husserl on the Moscow circle mainly to the efforts of Husserl's foremost Russian disciple, Gustav Spet, and describes Roman Jakobson's 1918 paper "Xlebnikov's Poetic Language" in light of concepts whose sources were Husserl (65). See especially pp. 60-9, <u>passim</u>.

[14] On Ingarden and J. Hillis Miller see again Abrams (133-5) and Magliola (107-41 <u>passim</u>) respectively.

On the confrontation between the Geneva School and Parisian

structuralism, see the chapter in Magliola, "Phenomenology Confronts Parisian Structuralism" (81-93).

On post-structural poetics, see the clear, comprehensive, up-to-date, recent work of Jonathan Culler, In Pursuit of Signs: Semiotics, Literature, Deconstruction (Ithaca, 1981) and Deconstruction: Theory and Criticism After Structuralism (Ithaca, 1982).

15 For this purpose I have used the 1965 translation by Richard Howard published by Grove Press (New York).

16 For a sample of the work by Abrams, see his "Behaviorism and Deconstruction: A Comment on Morse Peckham's The Infinitude of Pluralism" in Critical Inquiry (Autumn, 1977, pp. 181-93).

In his latest book, An Exemplary History of the Novel: The Quixotic Versus the Picaresque (Chicago, 1981), recently reviewed by me (Mentalités, No. 2, September 1983, p. 47), Walter Reed, in the chapter "The Problem With a Poetics of the Novel," refers to "open poetics" as "Aristotelian Poetics writ large" (p. 16), and proceeds to a historical approach to the novel.

Terry Eagleton's book, Literary Theory (Minneapolis, 1983), is a thorough survey of all recent trends in criticism, and a rejoinder addressed to radical disengagement from the real world.

In his typically cogent defense of structuralist semiotics (The Pursuit), Culler, while emphasizing that semiotics and the new criticism cannot be effectively ignored (an appraisal which is hardly contestable), nevertheless strikes a sobering middleground when he concludes, as part of his projection for a viable educational scenario for the future, that a liberal education should involve "an ability to see literature in relation to political, ethical, social, and psychological concerns, an ability to see literature in relation to other forms and forces of one's culture" (214).

GW01179316

Under the Blue Lights

Under the Blue Lights

My service with the Norfolk Ambulance
Service at Lowestoft Ambulance Station
(1974–1979)

David Sheldrake

Copyright © 2011 by David Sheldrake.

Library of Congress Control Number:		2011906592
ISBN:	Hardcover	978-1-4628-6420-1
	Softcover	978-1-4628-6419-5
	Ebook	978-1-4628-6421-8

All rights reserved. No part of this book may be reproduced or transmitted in any form or by any means, electronic or mechanical, including photocopying, recording, or by any information storage and retrieval system, without permission in writing from the copyright owner.

This book was printed in the United States of America.

To order additional copies of this book, contact:
Xlibris Corporation
0-800-644-6988
www.Xlibrispublishing.co.uk
Orders@Xlibrispublishing.co.uk
301972

Contents

This book is a lasting tribute to the Norfolk Ambulance Service and most of all to the men I served with at Lowestoft Ambulance Station, 'Under the Blue Lights' (1974-1979).

Former chief ambulance officer, Norfolk Ambulance Service: The late John H. Daykin. Former station officers: Mr A. Coleman, Mr B. Brunning, Mr R. Carroll, and Mr G. Ward. Leading ambulance men: Mr E. Eldrett, Mr D. Evans, Mr R. Knights, and Mr R. Rampley. Ambulance men: Mr J. Bond, Mr J. Sword, Mr T. Difford, Mr R. Worrell, Mr B. Barcley, Mr K. Rochard, Mr I. Levett, Mr D. Read, Mr T. Blowers, Mr T. Hall, Mr D. Waller, Mr P. Bradnam, and Mr J. Cobb.

I don't know what has happened to you all over the years!

But thanks for being fantastic workmates and making my time very enjoyable! God bless you all! And thanks to the former Norfolk Ambulance Service too.

Foreword

Back in the early 1970s, the NHS Ambulance Service came under the remit of the Norfolk Ambulance Service, and in particular, Lowestoft Ambulance Station, although clearly situated in Suffolk, was established under the same banner!

It was a local system and a fine workforce that worked very well in its day under the command of the late Chief Ambulance Officer John H Daykin. However, management and training and development requirements had moved on considerably.

Some twenty years later, the Norfolk Ambulance Service, more commonly known as the Norfolk Ambulance Service, joined with the Cambridgeshire and Suffolk services to become the East Anglian Ambulance Service NHS Trust. This was a result of government-required changes to the health system.

Then in 2007, the said East Anglian Service was reborn again after joining with Essex and Beds & Herts Services to become the (as we know it today) East of England Ambulance Service NHS Trust.

I, a little like the author of this book, spent most of my forty years growing with the relevant services, and the conversion from the recognised 'Miller Ambulance Aid' training into a 'paramedic' service has seen a vast improvement in patient care skills.

There will always be sad stories to tell—that's the nature of the 'job', but we must not forget the 'funnies' and the 'successes'—even the modern-day paramedics have to spend time alone because the 'wind' has got into their eyes or their crew mate has gone 'base over apex' whilst getting out of the cab at a RTC (road traffic collision).

I hope you get the 'feel' for some of this when you read on!

Kevin Janney

Ambulance Man 1971
Norfolk Ambulance Service

Senior Ambulance Officer or Resilience Manager 2011
East of England Ambulance Service NHS Trust

The very first emergency call

I joined the Essex Ambulance Service on 21 April 1981 at the tender age of twenty-one. I underwent training at Witham and in the first year completed the driver training and ambulance aid training, both of which were conducted at Markfield in Leicestershire. When all this training was completed, I was ready to undertake emergency calls, and as all new students, I was indeed very excited but nervous on what I would face dealing with people when they face life-changing emergencies.

I was pleased to be working with David as any new individual needed the experience and guidance of colleagues. I can remember sitting in the vehicle outside Southend Hospital when our radio was activated, and I was given my first emergency call. You hoped for something simple, straightforward that would settle the nerves and that would not involve all your new-found skills being brought to the fore on the first call. I was to be disappointed. The call was given as a gas explosion: An elderly person was involved. My mind raced as to what to expect and more importantly what I would do.

Dave was great; he was calm, professional, and experienced. We set off with Dave driving and me worrying. We arrived with the fire service.

There had been a gas explosion, but it was a small gas fire. The injuries were not life-threatening, and we treated my very first 999 call with Dave standing shoulder to shoulder, guiding and supporting. The patient was conveyed, and the emergency call went well.

I remember this call very vividly as it was my first call, and since then thirty years have passed. I have gone from that ambulance man to now ensuring we still deliver high-quality patient care across Essex as the general manager for this region. Over the years, I have worked with many new people, and that first lesson from Dave paid dividends as that supportive and guiding nature is invaluable to people undertaking this challenging role.

There were many other occasions I worked with Dave, and from that point, I have progressed and indeed am extremely grateful for those early formative years.

Simon Eatherton,
Essex Area Manager,
East of England Ambulance Service

Acknowledgements

First of all, a very big special thanks to my Jennifer! Without her encouragement and support, I could not have written this book. Another big special thanks to Kevin Janney of East of England Ambulance Service (Norwich) for all the help he has given me with my book. Thanks to Trisha Harvey of East of England Ambulance Service (Norwich) for all her kindness shown to me. Thanks to Simon Eatherton (Essex area manager) of East of England Ambulance Service for his comments about me. God bless you, mate. And last of all, thanks to the late John. H. Daykin, former chief ambulance officer, Norfolk Ambulance Service. Sir, thank you for giving me the chance to serve at Lowestoft Ambulance Station. A big special thank you to my publisher, Xlibris for turning my scribble into a book.

Chapter One

How It All Started

It must have been about 1971. I think it was when Jenn my wife and I decided to move from our one-bedroom bungalow in Essex to a brand-new three-bedroom detached house in Oulton Broad near Lowestoft, Suffolk.

I was only twenty-two years of age. We were moving to a new area. We did not know anyone there, and I did not have a job.

When we first moved to Lowestoft, the house that we were buying in Oulton Broad had not yet finished being built. So we had to stay in a very nice holiday centre called Broadland Chalets for four weeks or longer, if I remember right.

It was winter, and I needed a job, so I went to Lowestoft Labour Exchange (now called job centres). I found a job as a hackney carriage (taxi) driver with a company based in Lowestoft called Oulton Radio Taxis. Little did I know at that time how useful this job would be to me later in my life to have the knowledge of all the streets in Lowestoft and surrounding areas when life or death matters!

Anyway my first day at the taxi firm was very worrying, so was the first week in fact! The weekly wage was £13 per week plus tips!

I was given a black Ford Zodiac to drive, and I spent the first thirteen-hour shift in the taxi office worrying sick about being given my first job! At that time, there was no knowledge test for the area! Just fill out the application form, medical, and go to the counter for your taxi license and badge, and that was that.

Anyway, I sat in the cab office with the taxi radio controller; his name was Noey! And I was petrified of him; he was a very big person and a very experienced old hand at the taxi game! He had spent most of his years on the fishing trawlers out of Lowestoft. He used to speak with a broad Suffolk accent! And I don't think he had much time for young Londoners such as myself! But I have to say over the years, he became a very great friend with whom I had a lot of laughs. I will always have a great deal of respect for him. Anyway, there I sat on that first day in that small taxi office, in front of him, shaking like a leaf, when in walked another driver called Arthur. 'All right, lads,' he said, and then he sat down to watch the TV. I just sat there with a silly grin on my face.

Ten minutes later, the phone rang, which made me jump out of my skin.

'Oulton Radio Taxis,' said Noey Apter. After a couple more minutes, Noey said to me in his broad Suffolk accent, 'Job for you here, boy.' I thought, *Oh my god!* 'You want the Hotel Victoria, Kirkley Cliff?' *Chap is in the bar!* 'Do you know where that is?'

I replied in fear, 'Yes!' I did not have a bloody clue. I left the office, shaking again like a leaf. My nightmare was about to start! I got into the black Zodiac still shaking like a leaf, picked up the local map, and tried to find Kirkley Cliff: it was one of those old maps you had to unfold everywhere! And guess what! I could not find it on the map! *Oh my god!* I thought. I looked again, still not finding the road. Now panic set in. I thought, *Get away from the taxi firm! Make it look good!*

Problem number two then arose on the road: The Zodiac had column gear change. *Oh god! I've never driven a car with that sort of gear change before!* Panic set in. I was sweating very badly.

Then it happened. 'Calling car marks.' 'Mark 5, come in!' It was the very loud voice of Noey over the radio.

Oh god, Mark 5! That's my call sign! My hand was shaking when I picked up the mike.

'Mark 5 receiving,' I said.

Then again Noey's john voice came very loud over the radio in that broad Suffolk accent, 'How long before you are in Hotel Victoria?' *How long?* I thought. *I can't even find the road on the map, and I have not even tried the bloody car yet! I must get off the taxi garage forecourt out of sight first.*

I replied on the radio, 'Mark 5, about five minutes.' *I wish,* I thought.

I started the car and somehow managed to put in the gear! Don't ask me what gear it was, but the car drove off the taxi forecourt.

So there I was, driving this black Zodiac with the words Oulton Radio Taxis sign on the car roof and me the driver not having a clue where I was going!

I felt a feeling of both pride and blind panic.

It had now been some twenty minutes since Noey the controller had given me this job! The journey time from the taxi office to Hotel Victoria is seven minutes.

I was still no further advanced with it! I still did not know where it was! Again the sheer panic and terror returned! *What do I do? If I call Noey up for help, he will go into one and say why I had not asked for directions when he gave me the job!*

I said to myself, *Sheldrake, do you want this taxi job or not? Then get a grip, pull yourself together. I need money to pay mortgage and money for food, and we will soon be moving into a new house!* I saw a man walking down the road. I pulled up beside him and said in my London accent, 'Excuse me, mate! Please could you tell me where Hotel Victoria, Kirkley Cliff, is?'

I was greeted with 'Don't you taxi blokes take a street knowledge test?' How sad was that! He did in the end give me directions, laughing as he did so! I thanked him and drove off. *I hope he's right,* I thought, *and not having me on.*

Anyway, much to my relief, he was right, and I pulled up outside Hotel Victoria.

I got out of the car and went into the hotel bar and called out, 'Taxi!' Everyone in that bloody bar turned around and looked at me, and I felt my face go red, very red!

After a few minutes, a well-dressed man stepped forward. He said, 'Where have you been? I phoned for this cab ages ago!'

I said, 'But we are very busy, sir!'

He got into the taxi and said, 'I wish to go to Foxborough.' *Oh god, where's that?* I said to myself. I said to the gentleman, 'Sorry, sir, I am a new driver, and I don't know where Foxborough is. Please, could you be kind enough to show me?'

I was then greeted with these famous words: 'Don't you taxi drivers take a street knowledge test?' I thought, *Cheers, mate!*

He gave me directions, and when we arrived at the Foxborough public house, he asked, 'What the face on the taximeter is?' He then paid it and gave me a tip by which I was pleased with.

I had to call Noey to say I was clear at Foxborough. Before I did I looked at my watch; I had been on this job for one hour and ten minutes! It should have taken thirty minutes at the most.

Once again I picked up the radio mike. My hand was again shaking. 'Mks clear at Foxborough.'

Then came the reply, 'Return to office. Roger.' I thought, *Here it comes. Noey is going to go into one!*

I drove again onto the taxi forecourt and saw five taxis parked outside the office. I thought, *Great! I have now got an audience to contend with! It's going to be a laugh a minute at my expense!*

I got out of the car and was about to walk into the office with my tail between my legs when this broad Suffolk voice boomed out, 'Are you all right, boy? You Londoners love driving those Dagenham dustbins, don't ye?' He was referring to the car, of course, and me as a Londoner. He said his name was Bernie, and he was the petrol pump attendant! I said that I was a new driver called David and that it was my first day. I have to say Bernie was a very funny and a very educated man; he became a very good friend of both mine and my wife.

Wherever you are now, Bernie, God bless you, mate! 'And have you got a light, boy?'

I spent a few minutes talking to my new-found Bernie; he wished me well in the job.

Then I made my way into the office. I thought, *Let me get it over with!*

I walked in. Five other taxi drivers were sitting there. 'All right,' said Noey, grinning.

One of the other drivers said, 'Bloody hell! That must have been the longest taxi journey ever! Send a postcard next time!'

Another one said, 'What can you expect? He's a Londoner. You can't get the staff these days!' And they all started laughing. I could feel myself going as red as a postbox!

Anyway, I said to myself, *in future, if I did not know where the job was, I would ask the controller!* I spent the week working from the office, and confidence began to grow. I was learning the streets, pubs, clubs, and so forth!

I was unaware at that time about the next knowledge I was about to learn, which was going to be a very big asset to me at some future time in my life!

Oulton Radio Taxis had a contract with the NHS to transport blood and doctors to and from local hospitals in the area such as: Lowestoft General, Great Yarmouth General, and Norfolk and Norwich Hospital.

I found myself doing a great deal of this work! I used to have to wait at the hospitals to pick up the doctors' blood and so forth! I used to watch the ambulances coming in and out with their bells ringing. The thought never crossed my mind that one day I would be joining them, driving in and out, bells ringing, blue lights flashing! Anyway, that's to come!

I finished my week at the office, and the manager of the taxi firm said, 'Dave, you're OK. Now starting next week, you can start working off the Lowestoft Station taxi rank.'

That meant, 'You get work by way of three different ways: taxi radio, people coming off trains, and station taxi telephone.'

Chapter Two

Working the Station Rank, Local Characters

On the second Monday of the second week, I collected my taxi from the taxi garage; this time it was no longer the black Ford Zodiac—that is, Dagenham dustbin—but it was a brand-new red Fiat 124, one of twelve on the fleet! The roof sign said, 'Taxi' and the phone number, and at night, it lit up in blue, so it was a blue light! Was this an omen and sign of things to come? At the time, I did not know!

I drove down to the taxi rank at Lowestoft Station. And boy, was I about to see and experience life, both good and bad! And remember I am only a young chap of twenty-two years!

The first shock that greeted me was when I got to the station rank, there must have been at least twenty-five taxis on it! Lots of red Fiat taxis from my company! And a lot of taxis from another large taxi company called Ansells. Everybody seemed to know each other; it was like a large gentlemen's club!

I thought to myself, *How in earth am I going to earn money with this lot in front of me, and most of all, will they accept me as one of them?*

To my surprise, the taxi rank cleared quite fast as taxis picked up fares at the station door and over their radios!

As the morning progressed, I found myself getting closer to the station door! It soon became my turn to park on the cab bay by the station door! There had not been any jobs given out over the cab radio for a while, so there, say by the station door, ten, twenty minutes. Then the train from Ipswich arrived in the station. A lot of people got off it! After a few minutes, a very well-dressed middle-aged man in a grey suit and sheepskin coat and wearing hat came up to my cab and spoke in what I could only say a very posh voice, 'Good morning, young man. Please, would you be kind enough to drive me to Southwold?' Now I was a bit taken aback to say the least! Because Southwold is a little way out of Lowestoft and a good earner taxi wise!

I replied, 'Of course, sir.' And I called over taxi radio mks station to Southwold!

Anyway I suppose, we'd gone a couple of miles so, and my fare was making very polite conversation, and when I looked at him to answer him each time, I could not help but think I know that face. I had not lived in Lowestoft that long and did not at the time know many people, but I seemed to know him.

On we went, him still chatting, and by now his face was really bugging me! So I said to him, 'Sorry, sir. Please don't take this the wrong way, but I have seen you before somewhere!'

He laughed and said, 'I hope you have, young man.' He went on to say his name was Cyril Fletcher. Cyril was a TV garden presenter and part of Ester Ranzon team!

He was a very interesting gentleman to talk to, any the journey came to an end far to soon.

When we reached Southwold, he paid the taxi meter and gave me a very large tip and bid me farewell! And the taxi fare on the meter was a good earner as I said it would be.

As the days went on, I got used to worrying the rank, got to know the other drivers, and become part of the gentlemen's club!

One night, it was about 11.45 p.m. I was sitting on the taxi bay by the station door, when the taxi rank cab telephone rang! I got out of the taxi and picked it up! 'Can we have a taxi at the top of the town nightclub?'

I replied, 'Be about ten minutes.'

'We will be outside, mate,' they said.

Nothing unusual about that, I thought! So of I went and called job over the radio as usual!

Ten minutes later, I arrived at the top of the town club. Outside were two young men dressed in Teddy boy suits, which were the in thing at the time! They got in the taxi, all quite normal. Anyway, they asked me to take them to a certain public house in south Lowestoft. It was now midnight, and I really gave it much thought about the time, but the pubs close at 11.30pm.

Anyway, I took them to this public house, and when we got there, they got out and said, 'Will you wait there keep metre running?' I thought,

Oh no, you're going to do runner on me and not pay fare? What also worried me was, the public house was in complete darkness!

I had now been waiting quite a while, and the taximeter was clocking up a large amount of money! I thought, *If these guys don't come back, I am going to do a that explaining to the taxi go about this money on the metre and who is going to pay it!*

After a good forty-five minutes, these guys came running back to the taxi. They had asked me to park a little bit down the road. Again I did not give that much thought at that time. They got in and said, 'Drive off now.'

I asked, 'Where to?'

One of them said, 'Bloody anywhere!' I thought, *OK, I'd just drive after about ten minutes or so.* One of them said in a very calm voice, 'Driver, taxi us back to the top of the town club.' I did. When we got there, the taxi fare on the metre was by now a great deal of money! I pointed to the metre and said to myself, *Now the trouble is going to start!* But to my surprise and relief, they paid it! On top of that, they gave me a very big tip.

I drove off and thought, *Well, there you go!* I thought no more about it—that is, until a week later I read in the local paper, a certain public house in south Lowestoft had been robbed late at night! *Was it those two guys?* I don't know! But your guess is as good as mine.

Another night, I was on the taxi rank waiting. (I would like to mention that at this time, Lowestoft had a very large fishing fleet; it still has!)

It was about 9 p.m. when it came over the radio that first five cars on rank proceed to Lowestoft fishing trawler dock crew needed to be taken home in over words anywhere in Suffolk!

I was one of the five car drivers. When we got to the trawler dock, it was bitter cold, and you had to be careful as the key side dock was very wet! You slip into the water very easy if you did not have your wits about you. I was to experience this many more times to come in my life, only under different circumstances.

The crew was on the dockside when we got there. I had to take the trawler skipper who by now was drunk and smelled of bloody fish. If you get that smell in your nose, it would take days to get the smell out of your nose!

I asked him, 'Where do you want to go?'

He replied in a strong Suffolk accent, which I could just about understand, 'Er . . . er . . . I . . . want . . . go . . . er . . . home . . . Ipswich . . . but stop at couple pubs on way, boy!' I thought, *Oh god, no!* To crown it all, he had a lot of fish with him, smelling and very wet! There were cod, plaice, and mackerel. He said, 'Where shall . . . I . . . er . . . put . . . these, boy?'

I thought back, *In the bloody sea, I wish!* I said, 'In the boot, mate,' and that's where he put them! He got in the car, and I drove out of the trawler dock. I have now got him breathing whisky fumes all over me and this bloody fish stinking in the boot of the taxi! I called the job over the radio saying, 'Taking trawler skipper home to Ipswich!'

Now I did not turn the taximeter on. I would never do that, but something told me not to!

We'd been driving for about fifteen or fifty minutes then. It started. He turned to me, almost killing me with his whisky fumes again! 'Are you . . . all right, boy?' *Why do Suffolk people say that?* I thought.

'Yes,' I said, 'fine.' It was a good job I did not have to ask him the way! We would have ended up in tin buck to!

He said, 'Stop at the next village pub, boy!' I thought, *Oh god, no! It's going to be a long night!*

We stopped at the Spread Eagle pub in the village of Wrentham. We were just about to get out, when he said, 'Come on, boy, I buy you a pint!'

He must have drunk half a bottle of whisky to my one pint. After about an hour, I managed to get him out of the pub! I think the landlord was grateful to me in more ways than one!

I helped him back in the car or should I say he fell into the car? The smell of that fish in the boot and him was worse than ever! I drove off. We had been driving for thirty minutes. He had slept. But, oh god, he woke up! And then came those words again, 'Stop at the next village pub, boy.'

I replied OK.

We were over the side of a village called Saxmundham.

I saw a public house ahead of me. It had a thatched roof and looked like an ordinary cottage, but it had a pub sign outside. There were no car park, you had to park in the road, which I was not happy about it was pitch-black and no street lights! Anyway, once again he fell out of the car, and somehow he got into the pub! Then I got the shock: There was no bar, just a table with six chairs, and a large china jug on it! It was like walking into someone's front room.

There was no one else in there, just a very old lady standing there, it was like going back to Charles Dickens' time, which I fond a bit unnerving to say the least! It did not seem to bother the trawler skipper.

He said, 'I pint of beer for my friend and a double whisky for me.'

Well, the old lady poured the beer out from the large china jug into a pint jug! I thought, My god! she went out the back and came back with the whisky! I did not think it possible that a person could drink himself or herself sober, but that trawler skipper did!

By now, I myself had now two pints of beer and was feeling quite merry. So for him, he was becoming sober and still drinking whisky.

We stayed an hour or so, and he paid the old lady whom he seemed to know very well. She just put the money into her apron, and with that he just said goodnight and walked out.

When we got back into the taxi, he was normal. 'Do you know Ipswich area, driver?' he asked.

I replied, 'No.' I was a bit lost for words.

'Don't worry. I'll direct you.'

We arrived in Ipswich, and he directed me to his address. He was stone-cold sober, and it was 1.30 a.m.

We pulled up outside his house, and he got out of the car, and as I was getting out, he said, 'Thanks, but I can't pay you, boy.' I thought, *No, I don't believe this. It's like something out of a film! I am not going to argue with him, because I don't wish any trouble.* I just replied, 'OK!' *I am now in trouble with the taxi company.*

He said, 'I would pay the taxi fare into taxi office in two days' time. How much is the fare?'

I told him the amount, which I had made up.

'In the meantime, boy,' he said as he opened the taxi boot and took his stuff out, 'have these.' He gave me six cod and six tins of cooked ham. I just stood there. He then said, 'Oh, you can have this as well.'

He then took his Pilot watch, which was all the fashion at that time, off his wrist and gave it to me. He then said goodnight and walked into his house. I just stood there like some lost soul.

I drove back to Lowestoft to the taxi office and explained to the night controller about this trawler skipper not paying. He said not to worry, and I signed off duty and went home.

Two days later, I was informed the skipper did pay in the fare, which was the same amount I said, and would you believe? He left me a big tip! He must have been on the whisky again. What a result! But the taxi stunk of fish for days after, and passengers kept asking what the horrible smell was.

Chapter Three

Women of the Night and Sometimes Day

I had been on the taxi firm for a while now, and I was seeing life in all its forms. I was parked up at the station door cab rank one lunchtime when this lady came up to me. As she did so, all the cabs on the rank started sounding their hooters! At that time, I did not understand why! I later found out they were trying to warn me!

She got into back of the taxi; she was dressed very scruffy.

'Take me to north Lowestoft.' She said this with no *please* or anything.

I will refer to her as Ms R. She said, 'You don't know who I am or why those taxis are hooting, do you?'

I replied, 'No.' I thought, *Who have I got in the car? The bloody queen in disguise?* She said, My name is . . . , and I am a local tom' (i.e. streetwalker). A lot of the cabs won't pick me up.'

I said, 'Madame, I don't care who you are or what you do as long as you pay the fare!'

I was later informed that she used to go with anyone or anything, and she was none clean. She used to go around with an old lady whom I will refer to as Ms H most of the time. Ms H was always drinking day or night on the side of the road anywhere. Later in my life, I would meet Ms H again in very tragic circumstances. I was informed that Ms R and Ms H were very known local characters in Lowestoft for years, for the wrong reasons.

I did not pick up Ms R again. I made sure of that!

Then you had the respectable ladies of the night! Some of them had responsible jobs during the day, earning very good money, and then at night they did their second job, many a late shift a fare as got into my cab, with flowers and a bottle of wine. They would say, 'Please, can you take me to such and such a road and drop me at the corner?' Then when they had paid the fare, they would say, 'Can you come back in fours hours' time?'

When this went on four nights on the trot, it did not take long for the penny to drop, if you get my meaning!

Then there were the goings-on, or should I say carryings-on? The main work in Lowestoft was fishing trailers and oil rigs—which meant husbands missing for weeks at a time and wives becoming broads! Many a time, I have taken the husbands to the fish trawler dock, to the helipads to board helicopters, and to the oil rigs! Then in the night-time, many a time, I have taken males to ladies' houses whose husbands I had taken to work that morning! And it'd not been for a cup of tea! Many a time, the males have said to me, 'Have the tip, and you have not seen or know nothing.' Some weeks, I made a fortune out of them; it paid my bloody mortgage!

I am a cab driver. I work long hours. I hope my wife's not a broad!

During my time on the cabs in Lowestoft, which was three years, my father had been very ill off and on. He had kidney trouble and ended up having one of his kidneys taken away! And during that period, the hospitals and NHS had been very good and kind to him! And in some way I want to say thank-you to them. I was now turned twenty-five, still happy driving taxis, but the hours were still long, and my wife Jenney had just given birth to our first child Richard! I needed a job with less hours! One day I saw an advert in the local weekly newspaper—wanted ambulance driver or attendant to work shift timings by Norfolk Ambulance Service. I thought this as ways I could repay the NHS for helping my dad and shorter working hours for me! At that time, I did not give a thought to the sights I would be faced with or that matter deal with.

So I applied to Norfolk Ambulance Service, and they sent me an application form which I filled in and sent back! Well, the days went by, then the weeks, and then the months. I put the whole affair to the back of my mind and forgot about it. I carried on with the taxi driving; by now and all the time I had been with the firm, I had built up a very good relationship with the owners, Mrs and Mr Woods. God bless them! I could use Mr Woods's own personal car which was a top-of-the-range Mercedes-Benz for VIPs and airport runs! There was this one job with the Mercedes-Benz which was a very funny incident!

The taxi company had a contract with HMP Prison Service to take the prisoners and the escorts (i.e. prison officers) from Blundeston Prison to various London prisons. This particular day, I was given the job to take a prisoner plus an escort from Blundeston Prison to Wormwood Scrubs Prison in London.

I was allowed to take the owners' Mercedes-Benz, and I was dressed in a suite, shirt, and tie—suited and booted, if you like, as they say in London!

I arrived at Blundeston Prison gates about lunchtime and was let through the gates. Officers came out to carry out security checks on the car and me. I thought, *Blimey! Here I am sitting in this Mercedes-Benz, suited and booted inside the prison gates, with them carrying out security checks! They must have thought I was a London 'gangster'! Why did I not use a normal taxi for this job?*

Anyway, all was OK, and they told me to report to the reception office, which was hundred yards along the road, it was not a pleasant feeling inside that prison. I did not know at that time that I would be making future visits to that prison under different circumstances! Anyway, I pulled up outside the reception, and after about five minutes or so, two prison officers came out; they were about my age. Between them was a young male prisoner handcuffed to them. They got into car, and the officers introduced themselves. All the prisoner said in a London accent was 'Are we going to a bloody wedding, mate?' *Why did I bring the Mercedes-Benz on this job?*

Anyway, we drove back out of the prison gates en route to London and the scrubs. I think it took about three hours to get to Wormwood Scrubs in London; the prison officers had made good conversation on the way down, and I had got to know and like them quite well! The prisoner had said very little on the overhand. When we arrived at the scrubs, it looked a very forbidding depressing Victorian prison. We drove inside, and the feeling was even worse! This was a sunny day! What must it be like on a raining dull day?

We left the prisoner at the scrubs and made our way out of London back to Lowestoft. We were on the A12, approaching Chelmsford. It was about 7 p.m. when one of the officers said, 'Dave, is there anywhere we can stop for a bite to eat and drink? If so, well, treat you to a meal!'

I replied, 'There is a roadside grill restaurant about a mile along this road. I'll stop when we get there.'

At that time, this restaurant was called The Miami Grille; it was a bit upmarket, so to speak, if you get my meaning.

When we pulled on the forecourt, it was very busy and crowded, all the London city workers having their tea while coming home from work. Now as I said before, I had made good friends of these prison officers, and I turned to them and said, 'Boys, it's a bit crowded in there and we don't want to be hanging around waiting for a table for ages, do we?' Are you up for a laugh? I explained to them my plan, and they jumped at the idea.

Now picture the scene if you will: Upmarket crowded grill restaurant, no tables free or vacant, and crowded with London city workers, male and female, all enjoying their meals, when in through the door walks two uniformed prisons officers and me suited and booted between, handcuffed to them!

The customers must have thought they had got some London big-time villain with them.

The sheer stark cold look of horror on peoples faces! I have never seen a place clear so fast in my life, needless to say we found a table in very quick time! I don't think the owner of the place was none to be pleased! But the officers and I could not stop laughing! Thirty minutes later, I said to the officers, 'You can take the handcuffs off now,' and they started laughing again, (bastards!) Anyway, we had a very nice meal, made our way out, and said goodnight to the restaurant manager, but he took no notice. (I wonder why!)

We had a good journey back to Lowestoft, and I dropped the officers off back at Blundeston Prison. We all had had a good laugh, and I bid them goodnight.

The next morning, I had a very unexpected surprise: I picked up the morning post from the doormat, and amongst the post was a brown envelope; I thought it was a bill at first and was not going to bother to open it. But the postmark on the envelope was Norwich. I opened it. The letterhead read 'Norfolk Ambulance Service', and the letter informed me that I had been selected to attend for interview and driving assessment and that this would be in seven days' time. I could not believe it. It had been some five months since I had applied! I rushed upstairs to tell my wife Jennifer.

I went to work as usual that day, but after receiving that letter, I did not have much interest in the taxi driving. I could not stop thinking about the excitement of the ambulance service. But first I had to get the job and say the right things at the interview and not stupid things like, 'Well, I want to drive ambulances with bells ringing and blue lights flashing' even though I did!

Seven days later, I attended the interview; it was at 10.30 a.m. at ambulance headquarters in Norwich. A gentleman called Mr David Hewer interviewed me. He asked me different things and said, 'I see you are a taxi driver. Why do you want to join the ambulance service?'

I replied that my father had been in and out of hospital and that the NHS had been very good to him and that I wanted to thank the NHS in some way! I said that I also wanted a job that was a challenge and that I would like to help people.

The interview went on for an hour, and then Mr Hewer said, 'OK, I would like you to take a driving assessment in a few minutes. Just wait outside in the waiting room. Someone will call you.'

After ten minutes or so, a man in a suite came in and said, 'Good morning, Mr Sheldrake. My name is Mr Shorten. Would you like to take me for a drive?' He had a clipboard with him.

I followed him outside the building to the real yard.

Outside sitting in the yard was this large Ford Transit white ambulance, complete with blue lights and bell, with Norfolk Ambulance Service on each side of it, just like the ones I had seen rushing in and out of Lowestoft Hospital!

'Have you driven large automatic vehicles before, Mr Sheldrake?'

I replied, 'Yes, sir. I hold public service licence couch licence. I gained during my time with taxi company.'

'Oh, really?' was his reply. I don't think he expected that.

He said, 'Get into the driving seat.' Then he informed me about the vehicle. But I had known all about it because I had been driving transit minibuses. I just kept quiet!

We drove around Norwich City Centre and did rehearsing. He asked me a couple of things from the Highway Code. Then we returned to ambulance headquarters. I asked him how I had done, and his reply was 'Thank you, Mr Sheldrake. We will be in touch.' I felt so down and low in myself. *That's it, I have not got it!*

I went back to work as normal, still feeling very low in myself! Then two weeks later, another brown envelope arrived—not a bill!—from Norfolk Ambulance Service, informing me I had been excepted for the post of ambulance driver or attendant of Lowestoft Ambulance Station! Subject to passing a medical, could I report to Hall Road Ambulance Station in Norwich in a week's time for one week's ambulance injection course!

I was both shocked and excited on reading this letter. I was worked about medical, I was very, for but I don't like medicals. But I need not have worried. I passed my medicals and said thank you to Mrs and Mr Woods, the taxi owners, and they wished me well to start my new career 'under the blue lights' a week later.

Chapter Four

My Time in the Ambulance Service Begins

I reported to Hall Road Ambulance Station in Norwich at 8 a.m. on Monday.

When I arrived there, I was instructed to wait in the crew restroom, and I got a surprise when I walked in: A fellow taxi driver I used to work with at Oulton Radio Taxis, Mr Brian Barclay, was there! Neither of us knew we had applied to the same job! And he was starting at the same time as me! A few minutes later, three more new starters came in, two men and a woman; we all made friends and started chatting!

At 9 a.m., in walked Mr G. Shorten who had done our driving assessments!

'Good morning, ladies and gentlemen. Thank you for coming.'

We all replied, 'Good morning.'

He said, 'We would be with him for the week. After that we would report to our assigned ambulance service stations.'

At some time he did not know when we would have to attend six residential trainings at the ambulance regional training school at Chelmsford, Essex.

'And this would be a pass or fail situation. No second chance at it! If you fail, you're out of the job. As simple as that!'

I thought, *Charming! Nothing like being told from the word go.* I looked around the room and noticed the other new starters looking ill and white. 'However, if you study hard, learn the job, do as you are instructed, you will pass the six-week course. It's all down to you!'

He then said, 'We'll stop for a coffee break and then return to start our training introduction course!'

You can imagine the conversation during the break. It was a bit sombre to say the least! 'What had we let ourselves in for? Study?' someone said. I thought, *Only doctors had to do that!*

Someone else said, 'I have got three kids at home. How can I find the time to study?'

I said, 'I don't like the sound of "If you don't pass the six-week training course, you're out of the job". That sounds charming. I'll make sure I keep my taxi licence up to date just in case!'

Now the tea and coffee biscuits did not appeal to us anymore! We all went back to the classroom looking white and feeling ill.

Mr Shorten the instructor came back into the classroom, and he looked at our faces and said, 'My god, you all look as though you need an ambulance! Don't start worrying about anything because if you do, you best forget and go home now.' He then went on to explain to us what we would be doing for the next five days, which did not sound too bad! Afterwards we had a welcome to the service talk by chief ambulance officer, Mr John Daykin.

When this gentleman walked into the room, he gave the impression of being an ex-army officer. He gave us a very interesting welcome talk and made us feel we were needed. 'I don't know if you are still alive, Mr Daykin, but, sir, can I say it was a very great privilege to serve under you?'

Anyway, the five days passed very quickly. We learn to tie bandages, saw films on road-traffic accidents, learnt how to carry patients up and down staircases in fold-up ambulance carrying chairs, and had a lecture from the police and fire service regarding the road-traffic accidents! On the last afternoon of the course, we were all informed which ambulance stations we were going to.

Three of us were informed we were going to Lowestoft and the over two were going to great Yarmouth Ambulance Station.

I don't wish to bore the reader, but at this point, I need to inform you what had happened to the ambulance service just prior to 1974.

Great Yarmouth Ambulance Station was first run by St John Ambulance, and then it was taken over and run by Yarmouth Borough Council for a short period.

Now Lowestoft was St John's first, and then it was taken over by Suffolk County Ambulance Service. Now being the fact where Lowestoft is Suffolk Ambulance reply did not want the bother of Lowestoft!

At the time, the ambulance station was owned by St. John Ambulance Corps. There was no ambulance crew on station as such. If an emergency arose, the Suffolk Ambulance man on duty would drive to Lowestoft Hospital, pick up a hospital nurse, and go on to attend the emergency call. Not the best of situations! In 1974, things changed when I joined Lowestoft; Norfolk Ambulance Service took over the control of Lowestoft

Ambulance Station and Great Yarmouth Ambulance Station and made them twenty-four-hour stations and put in full-time crews.

On the following Monday, after my weeks' course at Norwich, I reported to Lowestoft Ambulance Station at 1500 hrs to join the late shift. The first thing that greeted me was: It was a very old building. It was the St John's drill hall and garage. The garage was very small. In the garage were two Norfolk Ambulance Service Ford Transit ambulances and St John Ambulance; they were parked in very tight.

I had not been given a uniform and was wearing normal clothes. I had been instructed to report to a Mr Reg Flux, transport officer. As usual I was feeling very nervous. I walked through the garage into a very small office. Sitting there was this very big man in his late fifties.

I said, 'Good afternoon, sir. I am David Sheldrake and have been told to report to you.'

He replied, 'Really?'

Now Mr Flux was Suffolk through and through and was not like the young Londoners. That I could see straightaway. He also had not liked the fact Norfolk had taken over Lowestoft.

I thought, *Oh no! Here we go again! I'd been down this road before a second no.ey!* He said, 'Go into the mess room and report to Mr Evans, the leading ambulance man.' And that was that! I thought, *Good start this is!* Anyway, I went into a very small mess room, and I mean very small rest room. It was no bigger than a large greenhouse! When I walked in, there were four men sitting there. One of them stood up and said in a London accent, 'Hello, you must be David!'

With a stupid grin on my face I replied, 'Yes.'

He said his name was Dennis Evans, and he was the shift leading ambulance man. He had a silver bar on each of his uniform shoulder. He introduced me to the three other men in the room. He said, 'This is my fellow crew member, Mr Roly Worrall.' He was about my age. 'This is the other crew with us on the late shift, Mr Joe Hamersley.' He was in his late fifties. 'And this is Mr David Waller.' He was a young man about my age. The other three crew members were all from Suffolk.

Dennis said with a grin on his face, 'I take it you have meant Mr Flux. Very stanch St. John's ambulance man he is! I would be riding on his ambulance with his crew member all week as a third man just to observe what's going on.'

At this point, David Waller said, 'Would anyone like a cup of tea?'

In this small mess room was a TV, settee, table, and two chairs, and a small kitchen at the back. On the side of this room next door was a very large St John Ambulance drill hall. Dennis said, 'As you can see, this is our wonderful living accommodation!' He then showed me around the very small garage that stationed the ambulances.

He said, 'Roly and I are the emergency crew for this shift, and we would be doing emergency work only. The other crew would be doing normal routine outpatients' work and normal ambulance calls, but they would do emergency calls if we were busy! Don't worry about anything this week. Just sit and observe. Next week you will be doing the work for real, including emergency work!'

Emergency work! I thought. *I have not got a uniform or been to training school. Yes, that should be fun!*

We went back to the mess room, passed Mr flux who said nothing, sat down, drank our tea, and after thirty minutes or so, then Joe and

David left to go to Lowestoft Hospital to store their normal ambulance duties. 'Cheerio!' they said. They said the same to Mr Flux, but I don't think they got any reply.

Dennis said, 'The time's our own now. We just wait for an emergency call from the ambulance control to come through to us.' Roly got up and switched the TV on. He gave me the newspaper to read and said, 'This room is not big enough for a dartboard or table tennis table like other ambulance stations have!'

At 1700 hrs, we were still sitting there. Mr Flux came in and said, 'I am off now' and turned round and walked out!

Dennis said, 'Problem with our Reg is he joined the service when it was run by St John Ambulance. Then Suffolk Ambulance took over Lowestoft for a number of years and gave him the position of transport officer. Now Norfolk Ambulance has taken us over. There's not really a position for him. They are just leaving him alone. He will be retiring in a couple of years! The trouble is the local hospital class him as the chief ambulance officer of Lowestoft Station! He was born and bread in Suffolk, and he was a very well-known local character! Poor Reg did not make retirement. He became ill and was forced to leave the service, and if I know Reg, he would not have been happy about that! He was in Lowestoft Ambulance Station! Reg, I don't think you're with us any longer! But wherever you are, you're always be in Lowestoft Ambulance Station! God bless you, Reg!'

At 1800 hrs, Joe and David came back in. 'Blimey!' said Joe. 'Haven't you three done anything yet? I bet David is bored stiff just sitting there!' And he said to me, 'Dave, relieve your boredom, put the kettle on, will you?' I had never drunk so much tea in my life! We sat there and watched the news on the TV.

Joe said to Dennis, 'Who is the night crew this week?'

Dennis laughed and said, 'Action man, ex-royal marine leading ambulance man, Eddie Eldrett!'

'What a man this man is! Ambulance man!' David said. 'And Mrs and Mr!' he said.

I said, 'Is Mrs and Mr husband and wife?' They all burst out laughing at me.

'They might as well be!' said Joe, laughing.

Mrs and Mr so-called were ambulance men, John Bond and Rickkie Knights, two smashing blokes you could ever wish to meet or work with! Mrs and Mr was just a nickname. Nothing was meant by it. No ill malice. It was because most of the time they were crewed together on the same ambulance.

At 2000 hrs, I jumped out of my skin; the telephone rang, the red emergency telephone. 'Here we go!' said Roly. 'Get ready!'

Dennis picked up the phone. 'Lowestoft Ambulance,' he said. Then he shouted out, 'Red call!'

Roly said to me, 'Come on follow me!' I really started to feel nervous now; *this is it what I had been waiting for I am now under the blue lights!*

Roly said to me, 'Pop in the back and sit on the seat near to us!'

Roly jumped into the driving seat, and Dennis got into the passenger seat. 'What we got?' said Roly to Dennis.

'Man has severe chest pains,' said Dennis, and he gave him the address. I knew straightaway where the address was and was able to inform Roly of its location.

Roly said, 'Thank God for having a taxi driver on board!'

On went the blue light, and the ambulance bell started ringing!

Dennis picked up the radio telephone mic and said, 'NorFam control, NorFam 186 mobile red to Oulton Broad!'

'Roger, NorFam 186. Your message was received and timed at 2008 hrs control out!' came the reply.

Wow! I thought we were going quite fast now, blue light flashing and bell ringing! We passed Oulton Radio Taxi office, and I could not believe I was on this emergency ambulance! In what seemed like minutes, we arrived at the address in Oulton Broad, a very worried-looking lady rushed out of her gate of her house to meet us. Dennis picked up the radio mic again and said, 'NorFam control, NorFam 186 on scene!'

Again came the reply, 'NorFam 186 from NorFam control. Roger. Your message timed at 20.15 hrs control out!'

Dennis picked a small portable oxygen cylinder and face mask and followed the lady into house. Roly said to me, 'Open the ambulance rear doors and wait there till he comes back!' He then went into the house. I felt a bit let-down; I wanted to rush into the house! *After all, I was an ambulance man! I should be in there!* But at the end of the day, I was not an ambulance man! So I just waited there feeling sorry for myself.

After about ten minutes or so, Roly came back out and said, 'The gentleman is not too bad! We will be using the carrying chair to bring out on!' *What the hell is that?* I thought. It's a folding chair with where on and caeying haudles top and bottom! Roly took hold of the chair from inside the ambulance rear door and said, 'Follow me and just watch what we do!' He introduced me to lady of the house and said, 'I was a trainer ambulance man.' And she wished me well in my chosen career.

Roly and I went upstairs to the front bedroom. In the bed was an elderly gentleman. He seemed to have a problem in breathing. Dennis had put him on oxygen. Again Roly explained who I was, and the man gave a wave to me with his hand.

Roly then said to the man, 'Sir, we are just going to put you on this carrying chair so we can carry you downstairs and into ambulance. There's nothing to worry about. You won't fall out. Just relax.' The man again raised his hand, but he did look unwell. His wife started to cry. Dennis said to her, 'It's OK. Don't worry.' They then sat the man in the chair, wrapped a red blanket around him, and strapped a best around him.

Dennis pushed the chair out onto the upstairs' landing. Roly stepped in front of the chair and got hold of the handles at the bottom of the chair and said to Dennis, 'After three! One, two, three, lift!' and they both lifted the chair and started to descend the staircase, one stair at a time. Dennis, who was at the top end of the chair, was facing the stairs and could see where he was going. However, the one who was at the bottom of the chair could not see where he was going; his back was to the stairs. He had to feel his way down with his foot on each; this all looked quite alarming to me.

All the time Dennis was saying to the man on chair, 'Just relax. You're doing fine.' It seemed a long time for them to get to the bottom of the stairs. They had to go very slowly. I thought to myself, *If I had been carrying this chap down the stairs, knowing my luck, I would have either fell down the stairs or dropped the person!* Little did I know I would be soon doing this something very soon myself!

Anyway, Roly and Dennis carried the man down the staircase and into back of ambulance. I could not help but think to myself, *How bloody fit they must be!* When in the ambulance, they placed the man on to the ambulance stretcher trolley, a sort of bed on wheels! Dennis kept the man on oxygen and then sat on the stretcher trolley opposite and instructed the man's wife to do the same. He asked me to close the ambulance read doors and the trolley as well!

Roly got into ambulance to the driver's seat, and Dennis told Roly to contact the ambulance control and inform them we were on route with heart patient (male) to local hospital. 'Know need for any blue lights!' he said.

Now the local hospital at that time was Lowestoft General Hospital! For reasons I can't remember, the ambulance control instructed us to take the patient to Great Yarmouth General Hospital some ten miles out of Lowestoft!

Dennis said, 'Sorry to the man's wife about having to go to Great Yarmouth General Hospital.' He picked up a clipboard and ask the man's wife details about her husband, age, occupation, previous illness, and so on.

After about thirty minutes, we arrived at Great Yarmouth General Hospital's casualty department. Roly opened the rear door of the ambulance, and I helped the man's wife out of the ambulance. Dennis and Roly unclipped the stretcher trolley and lifted it out still with the patient still on it.

They said to me, 'Stick close to them' and asked the man's wife to follow us into the casualty department. In we all went. Now remember, I am not in any sort of uniform! Dennis told the man's wife to sit and wait in the reception area. He then said to me follow us. We went through two double doors into canstry treatment area. There were doctors and nurses everywhere, all working and running about, patients lying on beds looking very ill!

Then it happened! It made me jump out of my skin! A very loud female voice shouted, 'Stop right there!' I looked around and saw this very large stern lady dressed in black with a white hat coming towards me! Well, I don't like to admit it, but I bloody started to shake! I looked around for Dennis and Roly, but they had gone! 'Get out!' she demanded. 'I am the matron of this treatment department, and relatives have no right to be in here!' she stormed.

I replied, 'But . . . but—'

'Get out!' she stormed again. I could feel myself going white with shock. Just at that moment when I thought she was about to get hold of me and throw me out, Dennis and Roly arrived back; they were laughing so much they had tears in their eyes! Dennis amongst moments of laughter tried to explain to the matron that I was a trainee, but he could not stop laughing! You know what it's like when you can't stop! I was not laughing; I was still in bloody shock! The dragon's response was 'All of you, get out of my department!' Well, we got outside, and Roly said to me, 'Your face!' and they fell about laughing again. I would meet this matron again in my ambulance career and cross her path! But that's another story to come later! Roly and Dennis folded the blankets on the stretcher trolley, and they then put trolley back in ambulance.

Dennis then turned to me and said, 'Dave, you can drive back to Lowestoft! If we get an emergency call, Roly will take over!'

I thought of not drive it! I got into driving seat of the ambulance very sheepishly. From the driving seat, it now seemed a very large vehicle—again the usual nerves set in! Dennis got in beside me and radioed ambulance control and informed them that we were clear at Great Yarmouth General Hospital and available for work. Roly sat in the back. Dennis said, 'Right, Dave! Let's go home!' I started the engine and pulled out of the hospital gates to return to Lowestoft Ambulance Station. After about fifty minutes, we arrived back at the ambulance station. When we went into the crew room, Joe had a mug of hot tea waiting for us; it was more than welcome!

Author when he worked for a taxi company

Lowestoft Ambulance Station, New One

Station officer Bill in white shirt and some Lowestoft ambulance men

Author in suit at Stansted Airport while at training schcol

Author second on right front tow with workmates at Lowestoft Ambulance Station

Author on right with Ken Hayward at Training school in Essex

Area Divisional Officer Mr B Carroll, centre;
with ambulance crews Lowestoft station

Beccles Ambulance Station
Large man centre is former workmate Mr Joe Cole. Officers in front are first
left, Mr B. Carroll and first right divisional officer.

Fakenham Ambulance Station Late 1970's.
Third from right Mr K. Janney who wrote the foreword part of the book.

Chapter Five

Leading Ambulance Man Eddie Eldrett Ex-Royal Marines and Alias 'Action Man'

The rest of the week I stayed working with Dennis and Roly. I learnt how to fold blankets, make stretcher trolleys up; learnt how to administer oxygen; learnt about Entonox, a pain-relieving gas; learnt how to use a carrying sheet, goals, and canvas stretcher; learnt how to use the scoop stretcher, which I would explain later on.

I also spent time washing, cleaning, and polishing ambulances. On Friday, Dennis informed that after the weekends, which were my rest days, I would be working late shift again and working and riding with a Eddie Eldrett and ambulance man David Waller. 'This would be an experience not to be missed!'

I had a very enjoyable two days' rest and on the following Monday reported at 1500 hrs at the station for duty!

Dennis and Roly were there, and two other chaps, Kieth and David, were on the early shift. Anyway, the late shift started to report for duty. First to come in were ambulance men, Trevor Difford and John Bond, to whom I was introduced to. The first words John said to me was 'I take it you're riding with action man!' And they all burst out laughing. I did not know what to expect. Then David Waller walked in, 'Afternoon, everyone!' he said in his broad Suffolk dialect. Then five minutes later, a man walked in: he was about thirty years old, not very tall, and all I can say is he looked like a Coldstream Guard. He was dressed immaculate. The peak on his cap was slashed: it came right in level with his nose! How he could see to walk I don't know! His shirt sleeves were rolled up, and he had tattoos all up his arms—a ship's anchor on one arm, the words royal marines wrote under the anchor and on the other arm, a naked lady!

Everybody in that room looked at me and laughed. I did not make any face movement. I just looked at him and froze with fear. Before we go any further, I would just like to say how ground I was to be given the chance to know this man and work with him. He was the nicest person you could meet, and he always made me laugh! Wherever you are now, God bless you, mate!

Anyway, in his broad London accent, he said, 'Aw right, lads!' But the way he told it, it made you feel as though you were in the army! Anyway, I was introduced to him. What struck me about him was he never took his bloody cap off the whole time. I was in the service! Even if he went to the WC (toilet), he wore his bloody cap!

After the morning shift, we went home, and we commenced our late shift. Eddie told us to go and check our vehicles and ambulance equipments. I went out with David, and he told me our ambulance was NorFam 187. 'Again a Ford Transit,' he said. 'We had been promised some new ambulance vehicles, but we are still waiting. We need a new ambulance station as well. This has got to be the worst in Norfolk.'

I asked him, 'What is in store for me?'

He said, 'Possibly within the next two days, you will become a crew member. I expect it will be yourself and Eddie! Also as you have been told you will go to six-week training course at a ambulance training school somewhere, but I don't know when that will be. It is hard there, but you'd get through it. If I can do it, you will! That's a matter of opinion I thought!'

He also said, 'By the way, don't laugh at Eddie!' We did our routine checks and then went back to the crew room. Eddie and David, with whom I was riding with, were the emergency crew for the shift that day. Well, we watched TV, while John and Trevor went out to do routine outpatient ambulance work; they would be available for emergency work if needed.

We sat there drinking tea and just chatting, and Eddie said to me, 'How you finding it?'

I said, 'I was enjoying my time here!'

He said, 'You were a cab driver, weren't you before? That's good! That would make your life easier!'

At about 1800 hrs, Trevor and John returned. We had not moved all afternoon! Trevor said, 'Still here, you lazy buggers?' They sat down and started to have their sandwiches and so on.

'I made the tea,' Eddie said. 'I am just going to do myself some beans on toast.' We all carried on talking and drinking tea. Ed came back in ten minutes and started to eat the beans on toast and joined in our conversation. We did not take much notice, but after he had finished, he did not say anything but got up from the table and went outside! After five minutes, he returned; he was carrying a small oxygen cylinder and was wearing a face mask and that bloody hat!

We all looked at each other, but no one said a word! He sat down at the table, put his feet up on the chair, and turned on the oxygen! We just sat there looking at him. 'Is he ill?' I asked. There was no reply from anyone.

Then after a few minutes, he starting farting (passing wind). Well, the smell was terrible; we could not stand it. We had to run outside! The smell! We were all laughing, and the tears were rolling down my face! Well, Trevor put on a oxygen mask and went and sprayed the crew room with a freshener! I had stomach pains, and I could not stop laughing! After a while when the smell had gone, we went back into the crew room. Eddie said, 'What's wrong?' And we all burst out laughing again! Anybody walking past outside would have thought it was the madhouse!

At 2000 hrs, the red emergency phone rang, making me again jump out of my skin! Eddie went and took the call, and after a few minutes, he shouted out, 'Red call!'

'Here we go!' said David. So we rushed out to the ambulance.

Eddie said, 'It's an RTA (road traffic accident), Beccles Road going towards Beccles Village!' Eddie jumped into driving seat, and on went the blue lights and the ambulance bell. David picked up the radio mic and said, 'NorFam 187 mobile red to Beccles Road!'

'Roger' came the reply. 'Your message timed at 2010 hrs control out!'

The excitement started to rise in me again. I was again under the blue lights, but I was worried at what we might have to face when we got to the scene! It was not but for some reason or another of this emergency seemed a long time getting to the incident!

Eddie said to me, 'When we get there, you and Dave can deal with it. I'll give you instructions what to do!' Bear in mind, I am still not in uniform!

When we arrived, the police were there. Already part of the road was closed off! It was the main Lowestoft to Norwich road. It was very dark. I could just make out a car hanging over a sort of ditch with a stream running along underneath it!

Eddie shouted to put the ambulance spotlight to shine on to the car. This I did, and it floodlit the car and the area. David said, 'Get the first-aid box and follow me!' I did. Eddie in the meantime had jumped on to the bonnet of the car (not the best thing to do) to give out instructions to us! He shouted, 'Just the driver in the car! Check breathing, bleeding, and other injuries!'

David got into car. By this time, the fire brigade had now arrived. I looked around; there did not appear to be any other car involved in the accident.

David shouted to Eddie, 'Driver is OK, just facial wounds and bleeding! No further apparent injuries!'

Eddie then said to me, 'What action are you going to take?'

I shouted back, 'Bandage and control facial bleeding and again check for any further injuries!'

'Right!' he said. 'Good, carry on! David' and I treated the man. Then we collected the stretcher trolley from the ambulance. We helped the man from the car; he was in a state of shock. We laid him on trolley and put a blanket over him. By now it was pouring heavy rain. We loaded the patient into the back of the ambulance. The last I saw of him was when Eddie was standing on the car bonnet!

When we had loaded the patient into the ambulance, David stayed with him, and I got out to find Eddie; there was no sign of Eddie or the car! I said to David, 'Eddie and the cars are gone!'

He said, 'What?'

The next thing we saw, firemen running to the side of the ditch! The car had fallen into the ditch and stream with Eddie still on the bonnet!

Well, you know what it's like when you have got to laugh and you know it's wrong to, you start coughing and try to stop yourself laughing! Well, the firemen helped him out of the ditch and stream. He was covered in mud and was soaking wet, and do you know what? Yes, you have guessed it! He was still wearing that bloody cap!

I have to say, I did learn a lot about the job from Eddie; he was a very funny man and always made us laugh, but what I will say is, he always wanted the job done in the correct manner!

Another incident was with action man who was on one night shift again; there was an ambulance man called Rickie Knights. When we were on night shift, we were not allowed to sleep, like the fire service do! But we did put mattresses down on the floor with a blanket and rest! But you dare not go into deep sleep!

Anyway, on this night, Eddie started his tricks again. Now on nights, Rickie used to take his trousers off before and lie down so as not to crease them and folded them over the chair, which he did this night shift as well! The mess lights were off, and we all lay down and dozed off!

It must have been about 2 a.m. when the telephone rang! Eddie shouted out, 'Red call!' John and Rickie were the first emergency crew on call! So john took details of the call from Eddie and dashed outside to the ambulance. The next thing I heard was bloody hell! Then all the lights were put on. 'My trousers! My bloody trousers! I can't find them! What bastards taken them!'

Eddie said, 'Come on, Rick! It's a red call! You must go trousers or not!' Eddie winked at me.

'I can't!' said Rick.

'For God's sake, go! It's a red call!'

Rick ran out to the ambulance in his underpants! Eddie and I were crying with laughter! Eddie then chased after Rick with his trousers!

Then they got out to the garage. There was John driving the ambulance out of the garage, blue lights going and Rickie falling about the driver's cab trying to put his trousers on and John cursing him!

Eddie and I just stood there, again crying with laughter! Needless to say when Rickie was on night shift again, he never took his trousers off ever! I wonder why!

The weeks passed, and I continued to learn more and more about ambulance work, but we new starters still did not have uniforms, which continued to make our life hard and frustrating. Requests were made to ambulance headquarters for uniforms, but only replies to come back no uniforms available.

I did manage to obtain a blue shirt, black tie, and black trousers, but that's all! I was in one evening shift when I was crewed with a Dennis

Evans; we got a red call. Dennis was driving, and I was the attendant. A lady was having a miscarriage (losing baby). We arrived at the address, and because I was ambulance attendant, I had to go in first and access the situation! I remember this call very well; when I went into the house, the lady was upstairs and a neighbour was with her. She was in a great deal of pain, losing a lot of blood from below and was crying! I asked her if she had lost any clots of blood. She said no and kept on crying! I stood there feeling very sorry for her. I had a first-aid box with me and said, 'I am sorry, but I am going to have to apply a large sanity towel and dressing down below to stem the bleeding. Please excuse me while I do this!'

The neighbour said, 'I will leave the room.'

I said, 'No, please stay. I would like someone else in the room when I carry out the treatment.'

I needed to safeguard myself in case the patient said I had touched her! When I applied the dressing, I had never felt so embarrassed in my life! I went back out and informed Dennis what was wrong and what treatment I had given. He said, 'OK, fine! Well done!'

We carried the lady down the stairs in the carrying chair. All the time she was crying aloud!

I said, 'It's OK, love. Everything will be all right.' But deep down I knew it would not have been.

We put her on the stretcher trolley bed and put the blankets over her. I sat on the trolley bed facing her. Dennis said, 'Check the bleeding every now and again.' By now she was looking very pale and white! She was still crying and in a very bad state! Dennis closed the ambulance doors. I asked her where her husband was. She replied, 'He's at sea.

He's a fisherman.' And she started crying again. By now I was sweating; it was a very warm summer evening.

I thought to myself, *For God's sake, do something for the poor woman!* I rolled my shirt sleeves up and said to the lady, 'Try to relax. We are going to take you to Yarmouth Northgate Hospital which is the maternity hospital.' The next minute, her pain got worse, and she cried out!

She then took hold of my right arm and started rubbing her hand up and down it. I thought, *Bloody hell! What's she doing?* I looked into the driving cab at Dennis, but he did not seem to notice. He just kept on driving.

After few minutes, I said, 'I am sorry, but I have got to check the dressing down below.'

She said, 'OK.'

I shouted to Dennis to inform him what I was doing again to cover myself! 'Everything is OK. The dressing is fine!' I told Dennis.

I sat back on the trolley bed opposite the lady, and again she starting rubbing my arm! I felt myself go red and started to feel a bit worried and embarrassed!

We arrived at the hospital, and the lady said, 'Sorry I rubbed your arm and embarrassed you, but like you, my husband has got hairy arms, and it was a comfort for me.' The poor lady did lose her baby. A terrible shame!

Chapter Six

Ambulance Regional Training School Looms Ever Closer

It was Xmas Eve 1974, and I was on late shift. My fellow crew member was ambulance man, David Read. The other crew members were Ray Rampley and Trevor Difford.

It was the usual routine shift, drinking tea, playing darts, watching TV, chatting, and so on! The time was 1800 hrs. The red telephone rang. David and I were the emergency crew members; David was the driver and I was the attendant. This emergency call would affect me for the rest of my life, even to this day, and I am now sixty-three years old! 'Red call!' shouted Ray. 'RTA, child involved.' *Oh no!* I forgot where the road was, but it was somewhere in Lowestoft. Anyway, away we went, blue lights and bells ringing! With this call, there was no sense of excitement, just worry and apprehension!

David and I said nothing en route to incident. On normal red calls, we spoke, but this time we did not.

It seemed to take forever to arrive at the scene, but it was not long really. When we arrived, there was a crowd of people standing on the road! David said, 'Oh no!' I grabbed the first-aid box and jumped from the ambulance while it was still moving! I ran to the small group of people who parted to let me through, and then there was this poor little boy lying on the road. He has about four years old! I stopped in my tracks with shock, horror that hit me!

David stopped beside me as well. For a couple moments we could not move; we just froze on the spot. I made myself move forward. I shouted to someone, 'What happened?'

'I don't know who.' But someone said, 'A car knocked him down and drove off!' It was so sad he was just lying there so still and motionless! I bent down over him; I could see the poor child was dead. David confirmed this as well. He then went to radio for police!

I asked some people where the child's parents were. They said, 'His mother's in the house opposite. She does not know about this yet!'

I then had to do the hardest thing I had ever done in my life—tell the mother! David said, 'If you like, I'd do it!'

I said, 'No, mate, thanks. I'd do it!'

I walked to the house. The street door was open. I knocked and shouted, 'Ambulance service!'

A lady said, 'Come in.'

As I walked through, there was the front room—an Xmas tree with all the child's presents around that Xmas tree ready to be unwrapped on Xmas Day! I just stood there and cried. So did the mother . . . She knew!

We took the child to Lowestoft Hospital mortuary. This spoilt everyone's Xmas and will haunt me every Xmas Eve till I die! God bless that child and his parents!

Xmas came and went, and life goes on in the ambulance service! Then in January 1975, I was informed that I had been selected to attend regional ambulance training school, six-week residential course in March!

I thought, *It's come! I could be out of a job if I fail, all those weeks of studying I am going to have to do!* I told my wife Jenney about the course; we had never been parted from each over before! But at least I would be home at weekends!

Those that had come back from training school said, 'It was not too bad, but it's all right for you lot. You've passed it!'

Through January and February, I started to worry about all; I liked the ambulance service and I did not want to have to lose or leave it!

Anyway, all to soon, March arrived. I would be going to the school with Joe Cole, another chap from Lowestoft Ambulance Station; he was a true Suffolk person, over six foot tall, about thirty-five years old!

Anyway, on the Monday morning, my wife took me to Lowestoft Railway Station. I kissed her goodbye, and she started to cry! That made me feel I was going to war! I one respect I suppose I was! I meant Joe at the railway station it was 8.30 a.m. the ambulance service had given us rail travel warrants!

I had been given an ambulance makeshift uniform cap, jacket, shorts, and a pair of trousers so at least I look the part!

We had to get the 8.30 a.m. train from Lowestoft to Ipswich, change at Ipswich for the train to Chelmsford, Essex. We were told a minibus from the training school would be waiting to collect at the Chelmsford railway station at 1030 hrs and take us to the training school!

The train pulled into Chelmsford at 10.20 a.m. We went outside to the front of the station to wait for the minibus. There must have been at lest 30 other trainee ambulance men waiting there, from Hertfordshire, Suffolk, Cambridge, and so on!

We palled up with two chaps from Suffolk who became lifelong friends to this day; they were Peter Wines and Kenny Haywood, and these two were to be very funny lads throughout the training period, and I have to say their humour and wit got me through the training school period whenever I was at a low period.

At 6.30 a.m., the minibus arrived and an ambulance training instructor jumped out and said, 'Morning, gentlemen! Put your suitcases in the back of the bus!' We all climbed in. No one said a word—I think because of nervousness of the unexpected!

Anyway, off we went. After about thirty minutes just the other side of Chelmsford town centre, we turned into this private road. There was a sign saying 'Essex Ambulance Service Regional Training School'. Pete from Suffolk Ambulance said just before we turned into the road, 'Look, lads, there's a pub there! That's handy!'

The instructor replied who was driving, 'You will have to finish your work first before you can go to the pub.'

Pete then said, 'Homework! Bloody homework! We are back at school!' I suppose we were.

As we pulled into the car park, we saw a large Victorian building ahead of us and lots of large buildings which looked like old hospital wards. Someone said, 'Bloody hell!' I later found out that before it was a training school, it was an old isolation hospital! *Charming!* I thought. *I hope they have cleaned the place.* We were shown into a large dinning room; there must have been some forty or more trainee ambulance men and women, all with their suitcases, looking worried sick! We were told to help ourselves to tea, coffee, sandwiches, and so on, which we did!

After an hour or so, ambulance officers came with clipboards and started to call out our names. My name was called, Joe's, Pete's, and Ken's, and ten others'. We were all together as a class for the whole six weeks and were known as red section; there were blue, white, yellow, and green sections as well.

The ambulance officer with the clipboard name was Mr Downing. He said he would be our section instructor throughout the course. He seemed a nice sort of chap, but he did turn out to be a very strict training officer, and at the end of the day, it was a good job he did because he got me and the red section through the course!

Mr Downing showed us to our rooms; they were quite small and were in one of the buildings that used to be a hospital ward! Pete said, 'Bloody hell!' in his Suffolk accent. 'I hope the place is not haunted!' We all laughed. I thought, *If it is haunted, after a week of us staying in there, the bloody ghosts would run away with fear!*

The rooms had two single beds and a desk and a chair, two small wardrobes, and a small wash basin. There was a shower room and toilet at the end of the corridor; later it was known to be the Rat Run, and I don't mean because of rats. You will later see why it was known as the Rat Run!

I had to share my room with my fellow workmate, Joe Cole, and this was going to be a problem. Pete and Ken from Suffolk shared the next room next door to us, and the rest of red section had the other rooms down the corridor.

Mr Downing told us to report in uniform in the main lecture hall which was in the main building at 1300 hrs (1 p.m.) for induction training. In the meantime, we got to know our fellow classmates in the red section, and what a lot of motley crew characters we were! All very young and, of course, like a lot of naughty schoolboys! And at the end of the day, that's what we turned out! How that training school turned us into professional trained ambulance personnel I'll never know, but, God, they did! We went there young and stupid but left there as 'professional ambulance men'! What a feeling of achievement!

We all attended the lecture hall, and the rows and rows of chairs must have been fifty at least! In front of us was a large long table with chairs behind it and blackboard to the left of it. A large film screen was behind it. We all sat down and started chatting. After ten minutes, an ambulance officer came in and shouted, 'Quiet, ladies and gentlemen! Will you all stand please?' Then in walked five other ambulance officers, all very smart in their uniforms, and they sat behind the large table. The ambulance officer who told us to stand now shouted, 'Sit!'

Joe Cole said, 'I am not a bloody dog!' This made us all burst out laughing! The ambulance officer glared at Joe and said in a very loud voice, 'Does someone have a problem?' The officers behind the table did not even smile! The ambulance officer said to Joe, 'Name please?'

Joe replied, 'Joe Cole.'

The officer seemed to have turned white. 'Stand up, Mr Cole.' Well, Joe was six feet eight inches tall, and when he stood up, it was like the Blackpool Tower, towering above the class!

Well, that was it. We all could not hold or contain ourselves any longer! We all burst out laughing, tears rolling down our faces! Joe by now had turned red with embarrassment. Poor chap! But the officer had now changed from white to red with rage, which all made us laugh even more! He shouted, 'You will be quiet!' At this, we stopped laughing, and you could have heard a pin drop!

He then turned to Joe and said, 'Joe Cole, what?' Well, Joe being from Beccles in Suffolk did not cotton on to the officer's meaning!

Joe again said, 'Joe Cole!'

The officer shouted, 'Joe Cole what? I ask you again.'

Well, Pete, Ken, and I were almost wetting ourselves; we had our hands over our mouths, trying not to laugh, but it was so hard not to! Someone whispered to Joe and said, 'Say "sir"' to which Joe replied, 'Cole Joe sir' to which everybody burst out with uncontrolled laughter.

Again the officer shouted, 'You will all be quiet!' to which we were! He turned to Joe again and said, 'Mr Cole, can I impress to you this is not a playschool? We decide if or whether you stay in your chosen career.' He then raised his voice and said, 'Do you understand?'

'Yes, sir,' replied poor Joe!

The officer then said to him, 'You may sit!'

He did not sit; he sort of fell back into the chair, making a terrible noise! The officer just stood there for a moment, just looking at him. Again we all wanted to laugh, but we dared not. The officer introduced himself as Mr Manley; he would be doing a lot of our training! I thought, *Well, we're all going to be in for a treat with him teaching 'us'.* We later found out he was one for the ladies, if you get my meaning!

He then introduced the officers at the table. There was our section officer Mr Downing, training school chief ambulance man Mr Solly, and training officer Mr Tripp. All these officers were employed by Essex Ambulance Service.

Mr Solly, the chief officer, stood up. He was a very young man to hold that rank. He said, 'Welcome, ladies and gentlemen! You all have a very hard task ahead of you over the next six weeks! You have chosen this career for which I have great respect for you all for doing this! However, we decide if you stay in this career, not the ambulance services you work for! It will be hard at times. There will be some fall at the fences. Listen to your instructors. Study in your rooms! There's only one attempt at the end of course exam. It's a pass or fail. There is no second chance to take it. We are looking for a pass mark of at least 80 out of 100! Remember—no pass, no job!' I was being told this in the year 1974. What must it be like in this day and age! He ended his speech by saying 'good luck, everyone' and then sat down.

We were all then handed a sort of programme explaining what we would be doing each day for the next six weeks and who would be teaching us. The ambulance officers got up and left the room, except for Mr Manley! He stood in front of us all and said, 'We would now have our first lecture on the role of the ambulance service.'

The lecture went on for two hours, at which time it was 1700 hrs (5 p.m.). He then said, 'OK, you can adjourn to the dinning room for your dinner. Report back here at 1900 hrs (7 p.m.) for another lecture!' We all thought, *Bloody hell, no!* We wanted to go to the pub!

We went to the dinning room and chose our table. There were Joe, Pete, Ken, and I on our table. It remained that way throughout the course.

All the officers had one big long table which they sat at for their meals. I thought, *Don't these officers ever go home!* The officers were always served their meals first and then we were served! The food was nice enough, but there was not much of it!

Because of the clowns I had with me on my table, every meal became the battle of waterloo! You had to eat your food with one arm protecting it! Because if you did not, someone would pounce at your pork chop, sausage, egg, or whatever you had on your plate at that time. You had to do this at every meal; it took about a second from 'Oliver Twist': more please, sir!

But this humour helped us through the course! As the weeks went on, we used to go to the local Fish and Chips shop or the local Chinese take-away for extra meals. We all returned to the lecture hall at 1900 hrs for an hour lecture on health safety and personal hygiene, given again by Mr Manley. After the lecture was over, we would rush back to our rooms, had a wash, and then Joe, Pete, Ken, and I would head for the local public house! Never did a pint of beer tasted so nice! The pub was fall of ambulance course members. I don't think the local pub customers were to keen on us, but the landlord was; the money he must have took each night over that six weeks! We left the pub about 11 p.m. We were not drunk but were a bit more than merry. We walked up the drive to the ambulance training centre, singing and pushing and shoving each other about and shouting out 'up with Norfolk Ambulance Service' and 'up with Suffolk Ambulance Service!'

As we got to the main gate, a torch was flashed at us! 'Gentlemen, please keep the noise down and retire to your rooms!' It was the ambulance officer, Mr Downing, still in full uniform.

We thought, *Has he not got no home to go to?* It turned out he was night-duty officer. *There would be a night-duty officer every night! Well, you would need one with us lot!*

Chapter Seven

Things That Snore and Go Bump in the Night!

We went into the corridor to go to our rooms, and the corridor was very dark. The only light was from the outside wall lights, which meant it was quite dark in there. Anyway, being the first night there and the journey from Lowestoft to the training school and the fact we had all been in the pub, we were all very tired! So we went to our rooms and fell in bed. Now as I have mentioned, I was sharing a room with my workmate, Joe Cole. I was woken up at about 12.30 a.m. by his very loud snoring! And was it loud! Pete and Ken in the next door shouted out, 'Bloody shut up, Cole!' and banged on the wall. At this, Joe became quiet and stopped snoring, and I and everyone else returned to deep sleep.

A little while later, I was again woken from a deep sleep, by Joe shaking me and shouting, 'Dave, wake up! Wake up!'

I sort of said, 'What's the matter?' It was now 1.30 a.m.!

'It's what they said,' said Joe.

'Who what said!' I replied.

'The place,' said Joe, looking very pale and white. 'It's bloody haunted! There is a patient from the past come back to haunt the corridor!'

I said, 'Don't be silly, Joe. You must have been dreaming.'

'Dreaming? Am I?' he replied. 'Bloody listen.' It was then that I heard a 'tap, tap, tap, tap' up and down the corridor. I could not believe this was going on! I again heard the 'tap, tap, tap, tap' along that corridor!

I said to Joe, 'We will have to have a look!'

I thought, *Shit! What if there is a ghost out there!* I started to sweat. I slowly opened the room door, and both peered out; the light from our room shone a slit into the corridor! I could see nothing or no one, and all was quiet.

We both started to walk the corridor. Ken came out from his room next door to join us. Others also came out of their rooms as well! There still was not much light in that corridor. We checked the outside door; it was closed. We checked the outside of the building; nothing or no one to be seen! We turned back into the corridor of the building. Then coming towards us through the darkness was this thing, all covered in white! Others behind us turned and ran! Joe and I just stood there on the spot in sheer terror!

I noticed Ken was at the side of me laughing. Then this thing came towards us, pulled a white sheet off himself, and there he, Peter Vines, stood tapping the floor with a bloody broom handle! 'You bastard!' said Joe.

Once the shock had left us, we stood there laughing so much. Ken went outside and told the others who did it. They did not find it so funny. We went back to our rooms, but we did not get much sleep after that incident, except that is Joe Cole who again bloody snored the rest of that night!

We were all up at 7.30 a.m., ready for breakfast in the dinning room at 8 a.m. Then there were the ambulance lectures until lunchtime and then mock ambulance excises in the afternoon!

Then after tea we went back to our rooms to do some studying, and that's how it went on that first week. Then back home to Lowestoft on Friday afternoon for the weekend and back to school on the Monday morning!

During the second week, I made a friend of a chap called Taffy; he had been in the Welsh Guards before joining the ambulance service, hence the name 'Taffy'. Now Taffy being a ex-guardsman had the peak of his uniform cap slashed, like a Coldstream Guard, which means the peak of his cap comes in level with his nose! When you're wearing your cap like this, you can't bloody see much because the peak is level with your nose! So in fact you are looking at the ground most of the time, but it does look damn good! I wanted this done to my uniform cap! So Taffy very kindly did it to mine! I was very pleased. I now looked like a double for action man Eddie Eldrett! I have to say he was very pleased when he saw I looked like him! As it turned out, Taffy did all the ambulance students caps on that course! But the instructors were none to be pleased! We looked like a bloody battalion of Coldstream Guards in the lecture hall! None of us could see where we're bloody going!

The second week at the school learning-wise started to become very much harder; the practical exercises, in ambulance work, the class lectures became more intense and a deal longer!

The second thing that increased was the fool's play with my fellow students in our dormitory section; I refer, of course, to that corridor or otherwise known as the Rat Run! At the end of the corridor was a shower room and bathroom; you had to be careful when you picked your time to have a bath or a shower! If had them early evening, you were wide open to attack! The same with early morning! I decided in my wisdom to have a bath late at night, when the Rat Run was dark and everybody would be asleep! I just had a towel around me. Joe was asleep in bed. I opened the room door without making a sound or putting any lights on. I closed it when I stepped out into the corridor. So far so good! I started to creep along the corridor. I must have been about halfway along it, when Joe started bloody snoring! The noise was so loud I just stopped where I was! Then it started: 'Bloody shut up, Cole!'

I panicked and started to run for the bathroom. I could hear doors bang open and laughing. The next thing was, the towel was pulled off me! Then the wolf whistles and cat calls started. I just threw myself into the bathroom and locked the door. I was shaking, but that's how it got you! Then came the banging on the door of the bathroom and Peter's voice shouting, 'We are waiting for you! You've got to get back to your room!'

Anyway, I had a bath but was unable to dry myself and was stark naked! I listened at the door. There was silence! I opened it a little bit—nothing, just darkness! But I knew they were waiting! A cold chill went down my back; I don't know if it was because me being dripping wet or fear!

I just had to make a run for my room, come what may! And it came. I started to run the Rat Run. I could hear doors open. I was hit with waste-paper baskets, books, you name it!

I fell into my room, dripping wet and sweating as well. I could hear the fits of laughter outside.

Joe was now awake and said, 'Are you OK?'

I replied, 'No, I am not. What did you bloody start snoring for?' Again I could hear fits of laughter from outside in the corridor.

At the end of the second week, there was a written exam; we had to take on what we had learnt in the previous two weeks! We were not given the results of how we did, which did not help matters!

The third and fourth weeks at the school were much the same but became even harder—further written exams to take and still not told the results!

By the fifth week, we had to stand up in class and explain the skeleton, all the bones and so on, the heart blood circulatory system, the nervous system, and the digestive system. By the end of all this, we all felt like doctors!

Towards the end of the fifth week, we were taken to Stansted Airport, Essex, where we undertook a practical exercise—a pretend plane crash! The airport fire service set fire to an old plane. It all seemed very real. We all had to undertake rescue procedures from the plane. It was all very exciting but also seemed real!

During that week, there was a very funny incident, which on this occasion was nothing to do with us! We were taken to the hospital mortuary, which we were not looking forward to!

We were taken into the mortuary in our section groups, each time by our ambulance instructors! In our case (red section), Mr Downing was our instructor! 'Ok, lads,' he said, 'in we go!' As we went in, we noticed the smell. There were large fridges and two trolleys with bodies, one of which was cut open and the third trolley had a body on which was covered with a white sheet!

There was a man in a white coat, who Mr Downing informed us was the mortician, a sort of doctor, if you like! He said to us, 'Gather around the gentleman' meaning the trolley with the body on it which was cut open. It was an old gentleman; looking at it shocked us a bit! The mortician then starting taking out various organs from the body and started explaining what they were. The smell was starting to get into our noses, and we all started to feel a bit sick and ill.

The trolley next to the body we were looking at was the body which was covered with the white sheet. While the mortician was giving the lecture, that body started to sit up on the trolley! Well, it was fear or shock of the unknown I don't know, but what I do know is two class members fainted! Half the class ran out of the room, but Pete, Ken, and I could not move; we just froze on the spot, feeling very ill!

Then the mortician and Mr Downing just stood there laughing! The body which was sitting up pulled the sheet off! And there was one of the ambulance school instructors! I have to say at this point, they attended to the chaps that had fainted! We just stood there still in shock.

That night, we went down the village pub and had a few pints. We were all still in shock. There were no problems on the Rat Run that night; everyone was very quiet. Even Joe did not snore!

The fifth week finished; we all went home for the weekend to return on the following Monday for the make or break of the final week! Either you would be in a job on the Friday of that week or you would not! Needless to say, the mood amongst us was very quiet and sombre. That final week, there was no messing about on the Rat Run, which I have to say I did miss!

We discussed what jobs we would do if we failed the exams this week. I said I would go back to taxi driving. Pete said he had been a taxi driver as well and would return to it!

That final Monday, Tuesday, Wednesday were just revision on all we had learnt. The final exams were to be on Thursday, so we all agreed on the Wednesday that we would pick numbers out of a hat! I think the numbers were from 1 to 50; whichever number a person picked, that would be his place to go and do the exam! We picked numbers in turn. My number was number 1; that meant I would be first in on Thursday morning to take exams!

We never got much sleep that Wednesday night, as you can imagine!

Thursday morning, we had breakfast and did not say much and afterwards went over to the lecture hall. 'here we go!' said Ken.

Mr Downing said, 'Who is the first candidate for the verbal test!'

I stood up and said, 'I am, sir.'

He replied, 'Follow me!'

We went into a side where the ambulance officer Mr Tripp was sitting behind a table. 'Ah, Sheldrake,' he said, 'I am going to give you an oral exam. Just answer as many of the questions I ask you, OK?'

I replied, 'Yes, sir.'

'Good luck,' he said and started firing questions at me. How would I treat certain injuries, questions on nervous system, digestive system, heart, and so on.

The oral exam must have lasted an hour or at least it felt like an hour! At the end, Mr Tripp said, 'OK, Mr Sheldrake, exam finished! You will now have to go next door and take practical exam.'

Mr downing shoved me into the room next door. There was a ladder against the wall and an instructor was lying on the floor dressed in overalls! And a training officer was standing with a clipboard. He said, 'OK, Mr Sheldrake, you're on your own. No one to help you. I want you to tell me what's occurred here and how are you going to treat casualty on floor and what for.'

I looked at the casualty; there was no exposed electrical wires, so it was not electric shock. There were no sign of deformed limbs or legs, but I checked them even so!

I spoke to him, 'Are you OK?' No response. I checked his breathing— he was. I checked for any bleeding—none. But he was unconscious! I turned him on his side, the recovery position! I then stood up and said to the ambulance officer with the clipboard, 'This man was up the ladder, had a stroke, and fell off there. Does not appear to be any broken bones, bleeding, but he is breathing but unconscious! Please, will you call ambulance?'

He replied, 'Thank you, Mr Sheldrake. Exam is over. The rest of the day is yours!' I went to the nearest telephone to phone my wife Jennifer to say I had taken the final exams but don't know if I still have a job!

I then went for a walk around Chelmsford High Street. That night, we had an end-of-course party at the village pub. The landlord who knew us provided sandwiches, cakes, rolls, and so on! We all got very merry and had a very smashing night. We returned to the school in quite a drunken state, and guess what was on that night? Yes, you guessed it!

The Rat Run started up again and various other stupid antics on that last night! School children again as it was on the very first day!

On that last Friday morning, we had our last breakfast! Then all over to the lecture hall to find out if we were still in employment!

Just as that first day, there were all the officers behind that big table. Up stood Mr Solly, school chief officer, and said, 'Good morning, ladies and gentlemen, or should I say schoolboys?' We got his meaning. 'I am delighted to inform you all that you have all passed! Well done!' We could not believe it! We were ambulance men and women! Real ones!

Chapter Eight

Ambulance Training School over Return to Lowestoft Ambulance Station

We were all very happy indeed when we passed the course: all the hard work had paid off! We all said our goodbyes and exchanged addresses to keep in touch, which is to this day! We then returned home to Lowestoft. Just before I started training school, I had to go to Burton's Tailors at Norwich to be measured for new uniform.

When I arrived back home, I was informed there were two new uniforms waiting for me! So I collected them from Burton's Tailors on Saturday.

On Monday, I started nights back at Lowestoft Ambulance Station, full of confidence and wearing brand-new uniform. Everybody welcomed me back and said, 'Well done!'

86

My fellow crew member was Joe Hamersley who was due to retire in a couple of weeks' time; he was a really nice gentleman. Everybody on the station laughed at my Coldstream Guard hat—that is, except action man Eddie Eldrett who thought the hat was wonderful! When we worked together, we looked like twins!

The week of nights started off very quiet indeed. For the first three nights, no calls were received, just played darts and table tennis. Then at 2 a.m. on the Friday night, the ambulance red telephone sounded!

Ray Rampley picked it up and shouted, 'Joe, Dave, "red call!"' This would turn out to be an incident I would not forget.

I got into the ambulance driving seat and turned on the blue lights. Joe picked up the radio mic and said, 'NorFam 187 mobile red to Kessingland.'

'Roger 187' came the reply. The ambulance controller informed us that the person we were going to attend was a male who was in severe depression and had very bad psycho problems, and this would be a section 21 removal, which means a could order has been obtained and the person has got to be taken to the hospital whether they wish to go or not! Not a pleasant job to have! They also informed us a (GP) doctor was in attendance, plus a social worker!

I turned to Joe and said, 'This sounds charming!' And we left the station and proceeded to a housing estate near Kessingland beach just south of Lowestoft.

Joe said to me, 'Dave, did the training school teach you how to deal with mental patients?'

'Not really, Joe,' I said. Then I thought back to the Rat Run! You could say that had been a bit mental! I suppose I had some experience!

We drove into a housing estate, all new nice-looking houses and bungalows! Not the sort of place you expect problems, not at 2.25 a.m.!

We pulled up outside the address. All the lights were on in every room in the house. Joe informed control we were on scene. He then said, 'On this one, Dave, we go in together!'

I said, 'OK.' Remember, readers, I am still wearing my silly hat!

The front door was wide open. We stood at the door and called out, 'Ambulance service!' Two men came towards us. One was Dr Osborne the GP and the other was the social worker, who looked like a hippy, with long hair, jeans, and T-shirt. Dr Osborne said, 'I gave the patient (whom I will call Mr X) an injection, but it does not seemed to have worked. You may have to use force to move him. He is very violent.' He then said, 'He is in the front room. Follow me, but watch yourself!'

We went into the room, and the sight that confronted me shocked and worried me! In the room, which was very nice, nice new carpet, furniture, and so on, was a middle-aged lady sitting on a chair crying! *This must be Mrs X*, I thought. Then on the other side of the room, standing by a glass cabinet, was he or 'it' should I say? Mr X was at least six feet eight inches tall, and he looked like Frankenstein's monster without the bolts in the neck! I thought, *My god, we've got big trouble here!* He was aged about fifty years. He looked down at me with eyes almost popping out of their sockets!

I said, 'Hello, Mr X. There's nothing to worry about. We are just going to take you for a nice ride.'

He replied, 'No, you're fucking not!'

I said, 'It's OK.'

He replied, 'Did you not hear me? I said no!' With that he punched the glass cabinet, smashing the china dolls inside!

I then said, 'OK, sir, you're not then!' I said to Joe, 'Let's go back to the ambulance!' The doctor followed us out.

The doctor said, 'You can't leave him! He's got to be taken to the psychiatric hospital. You know it's a section 21.'

I replied, 'We have no intention of leaving him, but we don't intend to get injured ourselves. We need assistance and backup for this removal.'

Joe asked control if the second crew at Lowestoft Station, ambulance men Ray Rampley and Kieth Rochard, could come and assist us, but the control replied that the second crew were attending another emergency call! Joe then asked for police assistance control to which they replied, 'Stand by!' After ten minutes, the call came back 'Police busy, unable to attend!'

'Charming!' I said. 'We have now got a problem!' Joe asked the GP if he would help us. He said yes, but the social worker refused!

Joe said, 'Well, there are three of us, but it's still not going to be easy! If we can get a blanket wrapped around him very tight and at least get him inside the ambulance, that will be a start!'

'It will,' I replied, not looking forward to it. We got a large blanket, and the three of us crept back into the house without making a sound! I thought, *I done this before! The Rat Run again!*

As we went into the room, Mr X was standing with his back to us—that was an unexpected result in our favour. We made a rush at him! But then the damn social worker called out to him! At that point, he turned around and came charging at us! In doing so, he knocked the poor doctor off his feet! It should have been the social worker he knocked over!

As Mr X charged at the doctor, we managed to get him to run into the blanket. I don't know how, but we got him wrapped up tight! It was like trying to hold a mad bull! The doctor was OK and administered another injection into Mr X through the blanket. It was now 3.45 a.m.; we had been at this address over an hour! We got Mr X out into the front garden; he was by now shouting out swear words and saying he was going to kill us!

By now, all the neighbours from the street had come out to see what was going on. We got to the ambulance rear doors; the doctor and Joe held the blanket around the patient so he could not break free while I opened ambulance doors. I then took over from the doctor.

As Joe stepped into the back of the ambulance, he had to release his grip on the blanket. At this point, Mr X broke free, and before I knew it, he had punched poor Joe on the chin and knocked him through to the front of the ambulance!

I thought, *No, Joe's due to retire soon! He does not need all this!*

Then Mr X turned and came towards me. I could feel myself shaking with fear, but I was also very angry indeed! I could see Joe's nose bleeding! I shouted, 'Stop it! If you intend to hit me, make sure I stay down! Because I swear I will kill you!' To my amazement, he stopped, turned, and sat on the stretcher trolley.

He said, 'Sorry, son. I promise I won't give you any more trouble.'

I said, 'I hope you're right because my warning still stands!'

As we started the journey to Yarmouth Psychiatric Hospital, Mr X started to talk. He said, 'My name is John.'

I said, 'Pleased to meet you, John. My name is Dave.' I thought, *Keep him talking*. I talked about football and all the rubbish that came into my head! I tried to avoid eye contact with him, but it was not easy; he had this very strange stare! The journey from Lowestoft to Yarmouth seemed to take forever! We did not put on any blue lights, because I did not want John going into one!

Now in the 1970s, these so-called mental hospitals were not nice places. They were old Victorian buildings, and I am sorry to say, full of lost souls, so to speak!

I found these places very depressing and very upsetting. We arrived at the hospital at about 5 a.m. It was beginning to seem a very long night shift.

I said to John, 'OK, mate, we are here now. You are not going to cause any trouble, are you?'

He replied, 'Not to you, Dave.'

It would have been OK except two male orderlies, as they were called then, in white coats rushed out to the back of the ambulance and opened the back doors and shouted out to John, 'Right out now!' They had jacket with straps on, which they intended to put John in, or so they thought!

I looked at John, and he winked at me! The pupils of his eyes got very big, and he stood up. His temper started up again, and he jumped from the back of the ambulance, and in doing so punched both male orderlies at the same time, knocking them out! Well, Joe just stayed sitting in the driver's cab. I was still sitting on the other trolley. I think it was more with fear than anything else, but I just started laughing, and John again winked at me and started laughing as well.

The two orderlies were still lying on the floor, I think for their own safety more than anything else! But it was not over yet as I was about to find out!

I stopped laughing and said, 'John, you've let me down! You said you would not cause any trouble!'

He said, 'I have not at least not to you anyway.' I was still sitting on the stretcher trolley. He was standing outside the ambulance! This was not a good situation to be in as he could now turn and run off!

I said, 'John, someone has got to take you into the hospital. You best let the hospital staff do it.'

He replied, 'No, Dave, I'll go with you on your own.' *No, this could turn into a very hostile situation—a violent mental patient and one ambulance man!*

Joe said, 'You can't do that, Dave. Not on your own. Think of your own safety! I call for police backup!'

I said, 'No, Joe!' I turned to John again who now again looked like Frankenstein's monster and said, 'John, look I am married with two young children. I will take you to the ward, but you must promise you will not cause me no trouble.'

He replied, 'I will not cause you any trouble, Dave.'

I went with John into the reception at the hospital and explained to the nurse who John was and what I intended to do.

She replied, 'You can't do that. You have to be escorted.' She had all the details on John! I explained to her that in this case it would be the safest and the best thing to do. I thought, *God willing!* For a few moments, she just sat there and said nothing! She then said, 'OK, I'll inform the ward you are bringing the patient to them. I will unlock the double doors which were in the reception area. You will have to walk down a very long corridor. You will see the ward at the end of the corridor! They will unlock the door when they see you coming!'

I turned to Joe who was in reception now and said, 'Make sure you have a cup of tea ready when I get back.' He grinned, but I could see he looked worried. The nurse unlocked the double doors. She put her hand on my shoulder and said, 'That corridor is quite long and the lighting is not very good. There are and will be inmates (patients) in that corridor. Just watch out for yourself!' She opened the double doors, and John and I walked through. What we must have looked like I dread to think, John over six feet tall and me wearing that silly hat with the peak coming down to my nose! All I could see was just the floor most of the time! I felt John hold my arm. I think it was a bit worried. He was not the only one!

As I have said, these hospitals were Victorian, and the first thing to greet us as we started walking that corridor was the smell of damp and the smell of urine.

I noticed there were no windows. It was quite dark, just light bulbs every now and then in the ceiling, but some of them were out! The corridor was very wide, and the walls and the ceiling went into a round sort of arch shape.

As we walked along the corridor, I had an uneasy feeling come over me. I could sense we were not alone! I could also feel John starting to shake. He then said, 'I don't like this!'

I said, 'It's OK, John. Don't worry!' I could not see or hear anybody, but I had the feeling there was someone there! I thought, *Oh no! Not a bloody Rat Run again!* Only this time it felt more sinister than the training school corridor!

We had only been walking a short while when I noticed people (patients), male and female, standing or sitting by the walls! Some were smoking (cigarettes). They were just looking and staring at us; they looked like poor lost souls. They were not talking, but some were making some sort of noises.

I could not see any nursing staff. I thought, *Why all these people up this time of the morning unattended?*

A middle-aged woman and man came close to me and started staring at me! Fear started to come on me, and I started sweating very bad. We just kept on walking, not making eye contact with them. It started to feel like a terrible nightmare!

I remember we were about halfway down the corridor. I did not dare look behind me, but I could feel something was not right! I could feel my uniform jacket being pulled from behind. John said, 'Someone is pulling my jumper.'

I said, 'Don't worry, John. Just walk a bit faster!' I could see the ward doors just ahead of us and could see nursing staff looking out for us!

I was now terrified because I had the feeling as if I was being pulled back from behind! I more or less flung myself and John at the ward doors, just to see the nursing staff in fits of laughter!

'What's wrong?' I asked.

'You should see your face! You're white as a ghost!' said one of the staff.

'Turn around and look behind you!' the nurse said, still laughing with tears in her eyes.

I turned around looked—a woman was holing on to my jacket. Behind her was a man holding on to the back of her dressing gown and so it went on in a straight line of twenty people or more! The nurse said still crying with laughter, 'We thought you were doing the conger!' (The conger is a party dance where everybody dances in a straight line.) I just stood there in a state of fear and shock, looking like the village idiot!

Anyway, the nursing staff escorted me back to reception area. Joe was there waiting with a cup of tea for me. He had been told of what had happened to me, and everybody started laughing again. All I can say is that tea was very welcome! Whenever I was working nights, I always made sure I wore black slip-on shoes! Because if a trick was played on you and if you were the first crew on call-out, you would have your shoe laces tied to together! You would be in such a hurry that you would panic because you could not get your shoes on; this would give your fellow crew members much enjoyment—at your expense!

One call we received while on night shift was when I was on duty with ambulance man Trevor Difford. We were called to a young lady who lived in Blundeston Village, about five miles out of Lowestoft. She had taken an overdose of tablets. When we arrived at the address, her mother was very upset and worried. We asked the mother, 'Why had she taken the tablets?'

She said, 'I do not know. She is upstairs.' We went up and called out, 'Ambulance!' We saw a young lady sitting on the bed. We asked her what she had taken. She showed us a bottle of tablets.

Trevor asked her, 'Why had you taken them?'

She replied, 'I can't get a man, that is, a boyfriend.'

Trevor replied, 'There are two of us here for a start!' She laughed. We took her to the Lowestoft casualty. I hope she recovered and found a boyfriend!

Talking of Blundeston, there is a prison there called Blundeston Prison, where in the 1970s, a famous member of parliament was sent to serve time; I think it was for some sort of fraud. His name was Mr X. One early shift, I was on duty with ambulance man David Read. We received a red call to Blundeston Prison Hospital unit—male with chest pains!

We arrived at Blundeston Prison main gate and were let through. Once inside the prison gates, the ambulance was searched by prison officers! When we were given the all-clear, we were escorted to the prison hospital unit through large iron gates with bar wire on top.

When we arrived at the unit, we went in and were introduced to Mr. X. He had, I think, either chest pains or stomach pains. We put him on the ambulance stretcher trolley during which point the prison staff handcuffed the MP to the trolley. We said, 'Is that really necessary?'

They replied, 'It has nothing to do with you lads!'

We loaded Mr Stonehouse into the ambulance and were informed two prison officers would be travelling with us to the hospital. We again had the ambulance searched and were given the all-clear and let out through the main gates.

When we came out through the gates, the press was waiting outside and started taking flash photos of the inside of the ambulance; we had to more or less drive straight through them! They followed us to Lowestoft

Hospital. I started to have a chat with the MP; he did not seem a bad sort of person.

When we arrived at Lowestoft casualty, the press was there waiting and started trying to take photos again.

That ambulance call turned out to be quite an interesting experience!

Chapter *Nine*

Ambulance Station Work to Rule, and Death and Dead People

During my time back on the station, things had been getting worse regarding the cramped living space and working conditions. Since Norfolk had taken over Suffolk, they had provided us with extra ambulances, and St John's were getting nasty about us using their premises.

We had kept asking Norfolk Ambulance for a better station; promises were given to us, but nothing ever took place! Enough was enough! We informed ambulance headquarters we would not use the ambulance station during the day whatsoever and that we would only attend emergency red calls! We would stay in radio contact with ambulances control, but we would park up at Lowestoft seafront!

This was OK for the first three hours or so, and then some Lowestoft councillors got wind of what we were doing and asked the police to move us on! We felt a bit like gypsy travellers; everywhere we parked, the police moved us on! But we stood our ground and parked on some seafront field at north Lowestoft. There must have been four ambulances parked up there. There was a tea place nearby which was very handy! This went on for three days, staying away from the station.

By now, the press got hold of the story and the Lowestoft journal newspaper and Anglia TV interviewed us! This really upset the ambulance bosses and the Chief Ambulance Officer Mr J Daykin and his deputy Mr Haque, who were both gentlemen! They assured and informed us we were getting a bigger ambulance station at Lothingland Hospital at Auction Village. 'So would you please stop this work to rule?' We did forthwith!

Talking of police, I have just got to mention one ambulance red call I attended! As I mentioned earlier, when I was driving taxis, I was caught in a police radar traffic by a young policeman by the name of Pic Allen (funny our names stay in your mind!). Again I was with ambulance man David Read when one afternoon we got an emergency red call to a private house on the Waveney Gardens estate, Oulton Broad.

David was the driver and I was the attendant. We arrived at the address. I was greeted by a lady who said her husband had terrible back pain. I noticed a policeman's cap hanging in the hallway. His wife took me upstairs to the front bedroom. On entering the room, I recognised the man—he was the policeman who had booked me some two years before for speeding!

'Good afternoon, Pic Allen,' I said.

He looked at me with a nervous look on his face and said, 'We have met before, haven't we?'

I replied, 'Yes.'

Then he said, 'When was it?' I was wearing my bloody, silly guardsman cap, peak coming down to my nose!

I stood there looking at him and said laughing, 'Who's got the power now and who's looking a bit worried?'

'You won't hurt me, will you?' he said. He was looking quite white; I don't know if it was because of his pain or seeing me!

I said, 'Could you manage to sit in our carrying chair so we can get you down the stairs!'

He replied, 'No, the pain is too much!'

I said, 'OK, Mr Allen, we will have to push you on one scoop stretcher!' I turned to Dave who was now in the room and asked him to get the scoop stretcher and Entonox pain-relieving gas.

Pic Allen kept saying to me, 'You won't hurt me, will you?' If he said once, he said it three times!

I said, 'No, I don't bear cruses!' and laughed. Dave came back after a few minutes. We put Mr Allen on the stretcher, strapped him in, and gave him some Entonox to help his pain.

He said, 'You're not going to carry me downstairs on this stretcher, are you?' There was alarm in his voice.

I replied, 'If you are in too much pain to walk, there's no other way. Anyway, we are very fit lads!'

We had to lift Mr Allen on the stretcher above our heads to carry him down the staircase. I could feel him shaking. He said, 'Don't drop me please!'

I replied, 'We only drop people on Thursdays.'

He went quiet for a few minutes. Then his wife said, 'But today is Thursday.'

With that, we heard a voice from the stretcher saying, 'Fucking hell!' We all laughed.

All the best, Mr Allen, wherever you are!

Well, to change the subject, I had been in the service for nearly two years and had not had much experience with 'death' or 'dead people' apart from that poor child on that first Xmas Eve—God bless him!

In most cases, death smells! It stays in your nose for days and weeks afterwards. The second death I experienced was at the cooperative food factory in south Lowestoft.

He was in his middle thirties, just fell down and died while working on the production line!

I attended the call with Dennis Evans. When we arrived at the factory, the poor man was lying on the floor, and what was so upsetting was he had his wage packet in his overall pocket! He had just been paid!

I think the shock of the man dying at work and just being paid had got to me a bit! In those days, ambulance crews had to convey dead people to casualty to have doctor certify the person was dead—as in this case. I don't think they do it this day and age. I think the funeral undertakers now take charge of all deceased persons.

Anyway, Dennis asked me to go and get the stretcher trolley and blankets. Now the factory manager and supervisors had not cleared the area of the working staff. Hence, there were about twenty factory women on that production line! I had to turn and walk past them; now I was only in my twenties and have always been a shy person (even now).

Anyway, as I turned to face these women, I could feel my face start to go bright red! They saw this from the start! As I started to walk past them, I tried not to look at them! I said to myself, *Get a grip, look down at the floor.* But by doing that, if I was not careful, I would trip over the bloody production line!

Anyway, it started: the cat calls, 'hello, darling,' 'I do like a man in uniform,' and so on, you know the sort of thing!

Anyway, I got out to the back of the ambulance, got the trolley and the blankets out, and started to return into the factory. I thought to myself, *Here we go again! Another bloody Rat Run!* And again it started: the wolf whistles, cat calls, and again I went the colour of beatroot, I heard one woman say, 'Oh, look he's getting hot flush!' I did not even know what a bloody hot flush was at that time!

When I got back to Dennis, he said, 'Are you OK? You look a bit red!'

I said, 'It's nothing. I am OK!'

We put the poor man on the trolley and put a blanket over him. This time when we walked past the women, they were very quiet, and their heads were bowed in respect!

We took the deceased to Lowestoft mortuary, where a doctor was waiting to attend the death. As soon as I entered the mortuary, I could smell the strange smell, which I can't explain. After the doctor had seen and checked the man, we had to place him into a large fridge! There were other bodies in that fridge!

Another death I had to deal with was with action man Eddie Eldrett. The deceased was a very large African lady; I can't remember anything about her death or where we got her from! But I do remember when Eddie was driving her to the mortuary. Eddie said to me after a few minutes, 'Dave, go and ask the lady if she is OK.' And like a bloody idiot—the penny did not drop—I went to go into the back of the ambulance to ask! Also on the way to the mortuary, the deceased kept farting. It was very funny and a bit unnerving at that time.

During my time in the ambulance service, I always found if you had one death, you had ten. It seemed to run in a pattern.

There was one death that stands out at the time, ambulance man Ivan Levett and I were called to a house in Lowestoft; we were called to a man. I don't remember who called the ambulance, but what I do know is, it was not his wife!

When we got to the address, our dear old lady came to the door. I said, 'Hello, ambulance service! We've come to see the gentleman who's ill.'

'Oh, my husband is fine!'

I said, 'Please, may I come in and look at him?' It was winter time and a very cold day! I followed the old lady into the front room. There was a big warm fire blazing up the chimney, and the room was warm. There was this very old gentleman, very well-dressed, sitting in front of the fire. He looked very comfortable indeed! 'I've been giving him orange juice to drink,' said his wife.

I said, 'Hello, sir, ambulance service.' He made no response. His face was very red, but he looked ever so well! But something was not right. I spoke to him again. Still no response. I started to examine him.

His arms and legs were stiff; he had no pulse and was not breathing! He was in actual fact 'dead'!

I said to the man's wife, 'How long has your husband been in this chair?'

'Oh, a few days or so, but he's not drinking his orange juice!'

It turned out that the poor man had been dead for a while! But because his wife had kept him warm by the fire, he looked so well. Poor woman! It was all a very sad affair!

Another sad death was, one Xmas morning, ambulance man David Read and I received an emergency call to the ladies' public toilets, London Road North, Lowestoft.

A female collapsed in the female toilets. When we arrived, police were in attendance. They informed us she was trapped behind a toilet door and they had tried calling out to her, but there was no response from her.

We all went into the toilets. There was a two-way gap between the toilet cubical door and the floor.

I lay on the floor and could just about make out through the gap a person in a sitting position up against the toilet door! I stood up and said to David Read, 'There's no way we can open this door from the outside. She's sitting up against it. I would go to the toilet cubicle next door and climb over the dividing portion.' I did, and as I climbed over, I could see who the poor woman was. I used to come across her a lot when driving taxis! It was poor old Setoch Helen, local Lowestoft character and local wine! Oh! I jumped down and checked her over, but she was dead.

I felt a bit sad when we took her to the Lowestoft mortuary. She was and always will be one of Lowestoft's, perhaps not the best characters, but she will be missed around Lowestoft.

The terrible thing with death, apart from the upset to people it leave's behind! It is that death smells. You have that smell with you for weeks afterwards! No matter how death occurs, you still have that smell! One of the worst times was when death used to upset me. If the patient died in the back of the ambulance while en route to hospital, I used to do everything possible to save a patient's life, but sometimes you were unable to!

The look on the wife's or the husband's or the relative's faces was terrible. They would say, 'Please, is there no more you can do?'

I always used to feel so helpless at these bloody times!

Chapter Ten

Fire, Police, Ambulance

During my time in the ambulance service in the 1970s, there was always the 'we are better than you' feeling between us, the police, and the fire service! The police were always the old bill, the fire services were the water fairies or boots and bonnets, and we were called the Cinderella services! I think this was because we were the poorer of the services!

Anyway, one afternoon, I was on duty with action man Eddie Eldrett when we received emergency call to attend a RTA at Beccles Village.

I was the driver on that shift. It was just about the time when all three services had done away with the emergency bells, and now had two-tone horns fitted to the vehicle, da da, da, da.

Eddie and I rushed to the new Bedford ambulance we had just been supplied with. I jumped in the driving seat and action man got into the seat next to me, and off we went. Eddie called control, 'NorFam 187 mobile red to Beccles.'

'Roger NorFam 187, police and fire service on route as well, message timed at 1530 hrs control out!'

Eddie said, 'This should be good.' He then switched on the blue lights and two-tone horns on, da, da, da, da; the noise was deafening—people in the street put their hands to their ears! 'Put your foot down! Let's get there first!'

I said, 'Bloody marine commando!' He laughed back at me! We had gone about one mile and were approaching Oulton Broad, when Eddie pointed to the water fairies about a mile ahead of us.

'Go on, my son,' he said. 'Bloody get past them buggers!' I was soon behind them, but at this point, I could not overtake; we were crossing over a narrow bridge over the Oulton broad river, Waveney! I was not going right up behind the fire engine. They were going da, da, da, da, and we were going da, da, da, da. As soon as we cleared the bridge, I started to overtake the water fairies. As we got past them, Eddie gave them riding gestures, and they gave the same back! Eddie was hanging out of the ambulance calling them names, and firemen were hanging out of the fire engine winding him up; he was having a right laugh.

I on the other hand was not; Oulton Broad is a very narrow village and at this time was full of holiday makers who could not believe what they were seeing, let alone hearing!

As I passed the fire engine, just in front of them was old bill (police) on the same emergency. Eddie was loving every minute of it. He must have thought he was back in the marines. 'Yahoo, yahoo!' he kept shouting.

I was, well, trotting myself; I was driving this brand-new ambulance which we had only had a few days! With this nutcase next to me and this other nutcase driving trying to overtake the fire engine and police car all at once in this narrow village, I thought, *Oh my god! What if something comes the other way! We will have head on crash!*

The noise was terrible: I was going da, da, da, da, the fire service was going da, da, da, and police was going da, da, da. People just stopped in their tracks and stared. Children got all excited!

It must have sounded like the Warsaw Concerto. The children must have been excited, seeing this ambulance overtiring the fire engine and the police car. I know the child next to me was! How I cleared that fire engine and police car without having oncoming accident to this day I never know!

Action man Eddie said, 'Bloody brilliant driving, Dave!'

Needless to say, we arrived at the scene of the RTA first! When we arrived, we saw that a car had crashed into the wall and two other cars had crashed head on! It was a major RTA. Eddie said to me, 'Treat the driver of the car.' I did and went towards the car which had crashed into the wall.

I could see the driver sitting upright in the car; in that day and age, you did not have to wear seat belts! But this driver was wearing a seat belt which I have no doubt saved the man's life! However, when I got to the car, the man's face was covered in blood. You could not see a face; it was like something out of a horror film.

He tried to talk but could not, and he started to panic. I said, 'Don't worry, sir. Ambulance service here.' I held his arm, and he started to calm down. I started by wiping the blood away from his eyes so at least he could see me.

He had a very severe open-head wound, which I treated. I then checked the lower half of his face, whereupon I found his lower part, where his mouth should have been, hanging off! Poor man was starting to go into shock; blood was pouring from the bottom part of his face, very heavy indeed!

Because of severe blood loss, I needed to think and act fast, but I needed help fast. I pushed the man's face together due to most of the heavy bleeding.

I looked around. Firemen were running in all directions. So I called to a large six foot of a man, 'Fireman! Excuse me, mate! I need your help!'

He came over. 'What's the matter?' he said.

I said, 'I need to get a dressing on this man's face. Please, could you hold the man's face together for me?' I was still holding the man's face together, and my kinds were aching and covered in blood! He took one look at my hands and the man's face and turned a horrible white colour and started to sway on his feet. 'I can't help you,' he said, and with that, he turned away and walked off.

I shouted, 'For God's sake, man!'

I was now in trouble. My hands were going numb, and my strength was draining, and I needed very urgent now to get a dressing on this man's face!

I had no alternative but to shout for help. A policeman came running over. 'What's wrong, mate?'

I said, 'I've lost the strength in my hands, and can't let go of this man's face! Please, can you take a dressing from my first aid and apply it tight to the lower part of the man's face?' He was very kind enough to do so!

After he had done this, I had a problem—taking my hands off his face: I had been holding the man's face for at least thirty minutes, and my arms had gone stiff! I had to ask the policeman to rub my arms to get the feeling back in my arms. Eddie was behind me and stated joking again 'Come on, Sheldrake, stop bloody messing about! A bit of blood won't hurt you!'

I got out of the gar hands covered in blood, feeling like death warmed up, but it's all part of the job as they say!

There was an incident which was worrisome but also funny afterward but not at that time. I was on duty with David Read. He was the attendant and I was the driver on that shift that day. We had just taken a patient to Lowestoft Hospital.

We got back into the ambulance, and David called control and said, 'We are available for work.'

'Roger' came the reply. 'NorFom 186. Proceed red RTA, Hopton.' Hopton is on the AR, between Lowestoft and Yarmouth.

On this shift, I was driving an older Ford Transit manual gearbox ambulance. I switched on blue lights and the two-tone horns, and off we went.

Along the air I went da, da, da. I was doing a speed of about 60 mph. We could see the RTA about mile ahead of us. The police had blocked the road with two police cars! I shouted to Dave, 'I get as close to the RTA as I can.'

'OK,' he said and started to get the first-aid box ready.

I had now started to get close to the RTA and applied the foot brake. Nothing happened there! 'Bloody hell!' I shouted. We lost the brakes, we were still doing gomph, and I was heading straight at the cars!

The policemen ran and jumped over fences and in ditches! I heard David shout out 'shit'.

I started to slam the gears through the gearbox: the engine was screaming by now, but we were slowing, but I had to avoid the police cars blocking the road.

I slammed it into first gear, pulled the steering wheel hard, left at the same time pulling up the hand brake! We came off the road on two wheels up the side of a grass bank, and bounced down again and landed up right.

David picked up the radio mic and said, 'Ladies and gentleman, thank you for flying with Norfolk Ambulance Service Airlines.' We just both burst out laughing. The bloody two-tone horns were still going da, da, da after coming off the road going up the back down and laughing back up right. However, the Suffolk police were not laughing as they climbed back over fences and out of ditches covered in mud!

We just took one look at them and just could not stop laughing again!

The people in the RTA that we were going to were not hurt, I am glad to say! When we attended to them, they were laughing as well. It was something like a scene from a carry-on film!

One further amusing incident was at Lothingland Hospital, where our ambulance was! It was one Saturday during a very nice summer, the hospital put on a hospital fete. I was on duty with ambulance man Trevor Difford, and we had an ambulance vehicle on display along with a police vehicle and fire appliance in the hospital grounds. We were standing by our ambulance trying to look the best of the emergency services! There was the usual jokes being drawn at each over between us and the water fairies, that is, the fire service. We were letting children sound our ambulance sirens, all the usual thing one does at these sort of events! The fete had been firmly declared open as these things are by a young, thin, long-haired gentleman. Trevor and I were standing, leaning on the front of our ambulance when the hospital secretary came up to us with this young long-haired thin man wearing a blue velvet jacket!

'Good afternoon, gentlemen,' he said. 'Please allow me to introduce Mr Richard Clayderman to you.'

Being young and stupid, we both carried on leaning on ambulance and replied, 'Oh, really?'

What a stupid thing to say to Richard Clayderman at that the time! If I had known our famous piano player was going to turn out, I would have stood to bloody attention! At that time, he had just one TV talent show; I think it was 'new faces'. Anyway, sorry, Richard.

Anyway, the hospital secretary said to Richard, 'These ambulance chaps do a grand job!'

I bet Mr Clayderman thought to himself, *I bet they do looking at these two clowns!*

Chapter Eleven

Maternity Cases, Unexpected Births

I had only been back from training school two weeks and was on night duty with John Bond.

It was 2 a.m. when the station emergency phone rang. Ray Rampley took the call and shouted out, 'John, Dave, red call! Maternity case for you! Lady getting very bad contraction pains!'

It was winter time and had been snowing hard. John Bond was the driver and I was the ambulance attendant. Now the only maternity training I had received at ambulance training school was of a lady giving birth and given a St John Ambulance manual! Great!

We arrived outside the address the road was a Couldie, 8 AC, and there was, I think, snow on the road!

John said, 'Go in and access the situation. I will be turning ambulance round, then I will be with you.

It was very dark and I was shivering with cold!

I knocked at the front door. Little did I know a nightmare was going to begin! The front door was opened by a man about my own age! I was greeted with 'Hello, thank God you're here! The baby's head is showing! Please come in quick!' I thought, *Oh god!* he showed me into the front room of the house there was a lovely warn fire going up the chimney and the room was very I warm in front of this was the mans wife laying on the floor! he rushed up to her and said, 'It's OK, darling. The ambulance service is here now. It will be OK now!'

Stood in front of her looking down at her the shivering from the cold now turned into shivering from nervous shock!

First I became very embarrassed that the mans wife was laying there her legs wide open showing everything to me! with her husband next to her! but worst of all the baby's head was now exposed!

I felt as though I was stuck firm to the spot my body would not move!

I then heard the husband speak, 'I expect you have done this sort of things loads of times!' I tried to reply. My mouth moved, but I could hear no words coming out!

He then smiled at me and so did his wife, so I must have said something, but I know not what.

What I did not know was I needed the maternity equipment box we carried on the ambulance.

I said, 'Hang in there! I need some equipment and the help of my ambulance man.' I went back out of the house to get John and the equipment.

When I got outside stark shock! No John no ambulance, I looked up down the road and could not see him! bloody hell I thought this is not happening to me its all a bad dream which I will wake up from in a moment! but I was awake and it was not a dream, and I was standing there getting covered in snow like a lost little boy!

I thought to myself after a few seconds for God sake get a grip on your self you are the ambulance service those people need your help now!

I rushed back into the front room, I said hi folks small problem nothing to worry yourself about!

Then something seemed to take over me I heard myself saying to the husband as the midwife been called! I felt very calm all the shaking had stopped!

But I could see the husband shaking still!

He replied he had phoned the midwife, I took my ambulance uniform jacket off and bent down in front of the lady and said hello my names David. I felt the heat from the fire on my back and I felt I was starting to sweat! But all my nerves went mad. I was very calm.

I asked if the lady was getting any contraction pains! She replied yes!

I did not have a bloody clue what I was doing, it seemed as though someone else or something was doing it for me! I just seemed to be going through the motions!

I took hold of the baby's head and supported??? it! and said to the lady when you start to feel the pains again start pushing hard.

There was still no sign of john but I did not seemed to be worried I just feet I had a job to do and I had just had to get on with it.

The lady gave one final big push and out came the baby a boy.

I made sure the baby was breathing and that the cord was not around the baby's neck, I looked at the cord it was quite long, I thought it needs to be cut, the lady must be got to hospital, I then started to worry again!

Then I heard voices. A lady said to me, 'Well done ambulance man.

I'll take it from here!', it was the midwife'

Then I heard John's voice, 'Well done, mate! You've done a great job!' I looked at my shirt; it was covered in blood and various other fluids! 'All in a night's work, Dave,' said john.

The baby's mother thanked me! I then turned to the husband and said, 'You know what you asked me earlier?'

He said, 'Yes!'

'Well, this is my first time!'

He then laughed and said, 'I would never have known!'

When we got back into the ambulance, I could not help but say to John, 'Where the bloody hell were you?'

He said, 'Sorry, Dave. I had a bad time as well. I drove down to the end of the road, to turn around, and there were a lot of parked cars! I got stuck in the snow and could not turn around. I had to knock people up to dig me out!'

"But what you moaning about you did not need me!'

'Didn't I?' I said. We both laughed, but that's one night I won't forget!

Some weeks later again I was nights again. It was the middle of the night! Again it was thick snow; that must have been a bad winter that year.

I was on duty with ambulance man Bob Carrall. He was the attendant and I was the driver. The emergency phone rang on the station. As I

said, it was the middle of the night as usual! Dennis Evans called out,'
Bob, Dave, red call for you! Maternity case!'

The patient concerned lived in the Beccles Village some miles out of
Oulton Broad. It was thick snow freezing cold, and I could not drive very
fast. it was hard and very slow going, I said to Bob by the time we arrive
the lady would have given birth! when we arrived the lady and her husband
were waiting for us, she had not given birth, but if was very close!

The roads had quite a lot of snow on them already.

We now had to take this lady from the Beccles Village to Great
Yarmouth Northgate Hospital some twenty-five miles away!

We got the lady and her husband into the ambulance and off I went.
The lady was starting to get pains as we loaded her in the ambulances.

As I drove off the snow started coming down very heavy, and it was
pitch-black drawing on the road between because and Oulton Broad,
plus I could not see through the snow! I could only drive at fifteen miles
per hour, I thought this is going to take forever, all the time I could hear
the lady mourning and screaming in pain, and bobs voice saying its all
right! he came up front to me at one time and said can't I go any faster,
I said its impossible!

It seemed like an hour when we were on the bridge at Oulton Broad
at the river Waveney when Bob called out 'stop!' I climbed into back
of ambulance, 'I need to push,' screamed out the lady. I said to Bob,
'Shall I ask ambulance control if Lowestoft Hospital could except the
lady owing to the conditions?' 'Good idea!' he replied.

I contacted ambulance control who in turn contacted Lowestoft
Hospital.

After a short time the reply came back Lowestoft Hospital unable to help because they are full owing to weather conditions and do not have a midwife or doctor available! Bob said blast OK push on.

It seemed worse than ever now the slow speed, the weather conditions, the poor women's constant screaming!

We were now on the A12 near Gorleston-on-Sea Hospital. We had been travelling one and a half houses, when Bob again shouted, 'Stop!' Again I climbed into the back of the ambulance!

I heard the lady saying, 'I can't stand it no more! I got to push!' I don't know how she had hung on for so long!

Bob said, 'Quick, give the lady some Entonox!'

Bob looked down under the lady's night dress, the baby's head was now exposed! The boor lady was ready screaming and crying.

We were twenty minutes from Northgate Hospital. Bob said, 'Push on, but tell ambulance control to have Northgate standing by! We have a problem birth coming in!' Ambulance control duly did this!

We arrived at Northgate Hospital some one and quarter hours later! A journey which on a emergency should only have taken some twenty-five minutes!

I am glad to say the lady was fine and had her baby.

But what a journey that was!

Chapter Twelve

Some Final Ambulance Memories

This book is nearly finished but there are just a few final ambulance memories which I would like to mention! One very said and the rest happy and funny. their was a very nice ambulance man by the name of George ward, he was a ambulance man at great Yarmouth ambulance station to start with. he then gained promotion to leading ambulance man and he was sent to Lowestoft Ambulance Station to take up his new position. all can say he was a very nice gentlemen! During his time at Lowestoft a very sad and tragic incident occurred which I will never forget. and the man never deserved it! He had a very nice wife who was, I think, a nursing sister at Gorleston-on-Sea Hospital.

She was always very nice to us ambulance crews when we took patients to her hospital. She always found time for a chat and a joke with us, always made us a cup of tea! A very nice lady indeed!

Then one terrible night (I can't remember if George was on duty that night or not. I think he was), a terrible tragedy occurred: George's house caught fire. I don't know how or why, but his poor wife died in that fire! Poor man, terrible! What a very nice lady she was! God bless you, George, wherever you are today, mate!

An incident occurred that involved another fire—and my mother! I was on duty one afternoon with Allen Coleman (aunty) as my crewmate. I'll never really know why I called him aunty. I suppose because he was like a mother to us! Anyway, this afternoon the emergency phone rang. Allen took the call! When he put the phone down, he was looking a bit pale and worried! He said, 'Red call, Dave,' I said. 'OK, what have we got!'

He said, 'House fire, lady injured! It's your mother!'

Do you still want to attend this call or shall I send the other crew!

I said no we will go, but I feet worried sick, I did not no what to expect! I should have been driver that day but Alan said he would drive!

We were at my mums house within six minutes! The fire brigade had gone! But her bungalow appeared to be OK no damage from any fire, that was something I thought! But out on the driveway burnt out was a galor gas heater bottle, used at the time to run a galor gas heater!

It turned out if it was not for young son Richard raising the alarm, and my wife Jennifer getting my mum out of the bungalow, because my mum refused to get out! But my wife got her out never the less! The whole place could have burnt down with her in it!

When I went into her house I found my mum sitting on a chair! My wife next to her and a neighbour all looking a bit worried and so was I.

I asked my mum if she was OK she said yes but her ankle and foot were in pain. I examined her ankle and found it was broken! And with

Alan put on a unflappable leg splint which we used at the time! And then we took her to Lowestoft casualty dept! And I was given rest of the shit off to stay with her!

I am very glad to say she was OK. a funny incident occurred one night shift, where I was to meet that hospital dragon of a matron again who had given me a dressing down during my first week in the service!

It was the end of my first year in the ambulance service, as I say it was one night shift, again my crewmate was ambulance man David read!

It must have been about 3 a.m. when the duty officer Eldrett shouted out, 'Red call, lads!'

Well, it was a man with chest pains and we had to take him to Great Yarmouth General Hospital, when we arrived at the hospital we were instructed to take the patient up to men's ward, which we did. it was about 4.30 a.m. when we came onto the ward with our patient on our stretcher trolley.

The ward was very dark and the other patients were asleep.

We could not see much before us just a nurse sitting at a small desk in the middle of the ward! The only light was a small lamp on her desk! She saw us and said, 'Please be very quite and follow me' she shone her torch as she went along, it was so dark and you could hear a pin drop! Well, it started didn't it, David looked back at me and started to giggle! well that started me off!

The nurse showed us which bed we were to put the patient in, we could not see a bloody thing let alone the hospital bed!

By now David is in fits of laughter! The nurse is saying ssh! Ssh! be quite!

Even the poor patient started laughing, which was a good thing!

Then the nurse can't hold out anymore; she started laughing.

With tears rolling down my cheeks, I said to the patient, 'We are just going to lift you off the stretcher trolley on to the bed!' I looked at Dave. He too had tears of laugher rolling down his cheeks!

I said, 'One, two, three, lift!' And we both lifted the patient on to the bed! That's when it turned into something like a carry-on film!

We had just put the patient into bed, and I turned around and walked straight into a large black oxygen cylinder bottle, which I did not see, knocking it over! I tried to stop it falling, but it fell to the floor with a loud crash and a bang! The whole of the hospital ward woke up in a state of panic and shock!

David just sat on the stretcher trolley in a state of serve laughter and crying with laughter!

The nurse said, 'Oh my god! What have you done?'

Within five minutes the double doors attend of the ward were flung open with a violent crash! In walked this lady dressed in black and wearing a long white hat! For a moment, in that darkness, I thought I was seeing a bloody ghost! But it was not a ghost! A ghost would have walked through the doors, not crashed them open!

It was that dragon of a matron whom I had come into contract with when I first joined the service.

She put the ward lights full on! There were patients out of bed in a state of panic! And the bloody oxygen cylinder was making a loud missing noise! It looked like a war zone, the patients were looking at me there faces deadly white and pale looking! On seeing this and the matrons face Dave could not control or restrain himself any longer, he was becoming ill with laugher! I myself just stood there like the village idiot.

'What the hell is going on in this ward?' said the dragon of the matron.

Then she gave a long stare at me and said, 'Oh, it's you again! It can only be you!' How she recognised me I never know. This was only the second time I had crossed her path! Also I was still wearing my silly hat with the peak touching my nose! So she could not see all my face anyway!

'Get off my ward, the pair of you! Now go on get out of my sight!'

I replied, 'Yes, matron.'

I had to help David stand up, because he now had stomach pains through laughing so much!

We said goodbye and sorry to our patient, but he was unable to speak he was crying with laughter!

David and myself both crept out past the matron if looks could kill we would both be dead!

When we got back outside to were our ambulance was, Dave and I loaded the stretcher trolley back into the ambulance!

Since leaving the ward and the dragon, Dave and I had not spoken any words!

But now we just looked at each other and burst out laughing all over again!

Another memorable incident I remember was when I was on a 6 a.m. to 3 p.m. shift one weekday. I think at the time my fellow crewmate was Trevor Difford.

Anyway we given a red call, it was to Blundeston Prison! we were just told male patient in pan! Not who he was! This incident took place 1976! Anyway Trevor and I arrived at Blundeston Prison main gate, and we were let through, the usual security checks took place.

We were then told the prisoner we had come to collect was in the hospital wing!

A prison officer escorted us to the prison hospital wing! The strange thing about this was as we made our way to the hospital wing we could he prisoner's calling and shouting from there cell windows and banging the cell window bars!

Trevor looked at me, a bit worried, and I felt the same.

The prison officer said its OK lads your collecting a high profile prisoner!

Trevor said, 'It's not some big-time London gangster, is it?'

The officer laughed and said, 'No.'

We arrived at the prison wing which was unlocked by a medical prison officer! He called us in, 'Hello, lads have been told who you are taking to Lowestoft Hospital.'

We said, 'no.'

I cannot give the gentlemen's name, but I will call him Mr X.

The officer told us who he was, he was a disgraced London member of parliament sent to prison for fraud at that time.

Mr X always had his secretary with him where ever he went even in prison!

How that worked or was allowed ill never no, but Mr X was a famous Mr!

She turned to us his secretary and tried to speak down to us!

But at that point prison medical officers took over! We but Mr X on the stretcher trolley and I asked him if he was still in pain!

In a very posh voice, he replied, 'I am OK, son. Thank you for your concern!' The medical officers then handcuffed Mr X to the stretcher trolley both his arms.

I said to one of the prison officers, 'Is that really necessary?'

He replied, 'You do your job, and we will do ours'

I replied, 'That's just it. With this patient's arms both handcuffed, I can't do my job! I need to check his pulse en route and other medical checks.'

The prison officer said, 'That's your hard luck and Mr X's hard luck as well!'

I was now starting to get angry I said, 'Look here he may be a high profile prisoner in your care' but when in our care he becomes a medical patient who may need medical aid! the officer replied no we will give him medical aid if he needs any!

I replied in a raised voice, 'The minute this gentleman is placed in our ambulance, he becomes the responsibility of the ambulance crew and Norfolk Ambulance Service unless you are a doctor or a medical surgeon who will take full responsibility!

His fellow officer said, 'Leave it, John. Let the ambulance lads do their job!'

He then turned to me and said, 'I will uncuff one of his arms, will you except that?'

I replied, 'Thank you!'

We put Mr X and his prison officers and Mrs Secretary into the ambulance. The usual security checks were again carried out at the prison gate only more intense this time.

On the way to Lowestoft Hospital I kept checking Mr X's pulse, breathing, and so on.

He was a very nice gentleman to talk to and I had a very interesting conversation with him. the prison officers however said nothing the whole duration of the journey!

We arrived at Lowestoft Hospital and took Mr X to the ward and into a private side room. The officers uncuffed Mr X's arm from the stretcher trolley.

Mr X stood up shook our hands and said, 'Thank you very much, gentlemen, for your kindness' and winked at us!

His secretary also changed her attitude toward us and said, 'Thank you.'

The prison officers well they said nothing. make of that what you will.

Epilogue

Well, this book is almost at its end.

I left Norfolk Ambulance Service and Lowestoft Ambulance Station with great sadness in late 1979.

The lads from Lowestoft Ambulance gave me a surprise leaving party at Blue Boar Public House, Oulton Village. I have to say I got a bit drunk that night and spent most of the night sleeping on my front room floor! I think the reason I left the service was because my wife and I purchased a pet-shop business in high Wycombe Bucks! But, boy, did I miss Norfolk Ambulance!

My daughter Angelique, was St John's nursing cadet. She lived and died for St John! She, at one time, became nursing cadet of the year!

When she started work, she trained to be a hairdresser, but she really wanted nursing as a job.

She trained at Orsett Hospital to be a nurse; she really worked hard at it, and to this day some twenty years or so on, she is a nurse at the Mayday Hospital, Croydon, Surrey.

Well done to her! I am very proud of her.

After a year or so, we sold the pet shop and moved back to Canvey Island. I joined a private ambulance service in London, called EMS private ambulance service run by Mrs J Stowell (srn) and Mr J Stowell, referred to at all times as (governor) and Mrs Stowell as (sister). I worked for them for a few years, which I enjoyed. All the best to you, Janet and Joe!

I am now sixty-four years of age. I have enjoyed writing this book, and this has book many fond memories!

The men at Lowestoft Ambulance were more than friends, more than workmates! They were comrades through and through. Well, we were not like the hi-tec paramedics of 'today'.

But we did our best, gave our all under all conditions and 'under the blue lights'. We did save lives . . . didn't we, lads? I like to think former chief ambulance officer, Mr John Daykin, was proud of us at Lowestoft Ambulance Station, as he would have been of all his ambulance stations in Norfolk.

God rest his soul.

Lightning Source UK Ltd.
Milton Keynes UK
175956UK00002B/7/P